SATANISM:
THE TRUTH BEHIND THE VEIL

UNFOLDING THE DARKNESS

SATANISM:
THE TRUTH BEHIND THE VEIL

UNFOLDING THE DARKNESS

ANGELA GREENIG

Generation Culture Transformation
Specializing in publishing for generation culture change

eGenCo. LLC
824 Tallow Hill Road
Chambersburg, PA 17202, USA
Phone: 717-461-3436
email: info@egen.co
Website: www.egen.co
                www.goingebook.com

 facebook.com/egenbooks

 youtube.com/egenpub

 egen.co/blog

Previously published by:
Angela Greenig Ministries
SetFree Ministries International

Printed 2010

Publisher's Cataloging-in-Publication Data
Greenig, Angela
        Satanism: The truth behind the veil. Unfolding the darkness/Angela Greennig;
        p.cm.
        ISBN: 978-1-936554-33-1 paperback
               978-1-936554-34-8 ebook
               978-1-936554-35-5 ebook
        1. Religion. 2. Christian life. 3. Satan I. Title
                        2013934905

ACKNOWLEDGMENTS

For Larry, Chad, Wendy and Robert—my wonderful husband and awesome kids: You are my superheroes. I am so moved by you. You have such a passion and compassion for the Lord and for ministry. I love watching you care for the poor. I love that we all can work together for the Kingdom, and it has been amazing to realize how each of our individual giftings complement one another. Thank you for your patience and your years of loving me through the valley of the shadow of death. You have loved me through the heartache and pain. Thank you for standing with me and praying me through; thank you for helping me birth the ministries that now catapult all over the world. I could not have done this without you.

ENDORSEMENTS

Angela has rescued many people out of darkness. I thank Jesus for a woman who intercedes for those in darkness to come into the glorious salvation and light of Christ Jesus.

Heidi Baker, Ph.D.
Founding Director
Iris Ministries, Inc.

Satanism: The Truth Behind the Veil is nothing short of eye-opening. It brings such deep awareness of how far the enemy will reach to dispel hope, while revealing battle strategies on how to reclaim that which belongs to the Lord. If you want to be empowered to release light into the darkest places, this book is for you.

Wendy Greenig Bearden
Enthrone Worship Ministries
iEnthrone.org

My generation is looking for supernatural answers to supernatural questions. *Satanism: The Truth Behind the Veil* gives us those answers that allow us to overcome our adversary in very real and tangible ways. Angela Greenig is a forerunner revealing how to war and win against the enemy like never before.

Anny Donewald
Eve's Angels
www.EvesAngels.org

I know few warriors like Angela Greenig. She connects to the revelation of the cross and releases the Kingdom of God with a great authority that comes from many battles and many victories. Not always understood by man, but deeply set in the heart of God, this "warrior woman" has much to share.

As you read, you will learn many of the strategies of the enemy against you and the Church in this hour. You will find out about demonic rites, rituals, and hierarchies, and gain faith that the finished work of the cross is greater than them all! Angela's great desire is to help every believer increase in discernment and understanding of what the plots and ploys of the enemy are, so that we may operate against them in greater effectiveness. What you encounter in these pages will more than likely stretch you, challenge you, and even shock you. This manual is not for the faint of heart, but it is for those who long to see the rule and reign of Jesus Christ established in the earth in all places and all situations. Scripture tells us that God's people perish for lack of knowledge. *Satanism: The Truth Behind the Veil* will help you gain knowledge of how the enemy releases his darkness into the earth, and how you can counter and destroy that darkness through the light and truth of Jesus Christ!

Rob Hotchkin
Extreme Prophetic
XPmedia.com

God is looking for a people who will make a choice. He is looking for a people who are sold out for Him. He wants good things for us; He wants our hearts to be discerning. His desire is for us to not be deceived by the enemy but for us to see the deception for what it is. He says my people die for lack of knowledge. Angela's book is full of information to train us in recognizing the tactics; tactics that have been so subtle that it has successfully deceived generations. Satan's job is to steal, kill, and destroy and we must be on guard, we must be watchmen and women to recognize the signs of the times and avoid the entrapments of the enemy.

Marti Statler
eGenCo

We are living in a historical moment in the history of mankind. Just recently, God spoke to my heart about the days we are living in. The earth is on the fast track to the end of the age. The ancient prophets of the Old Testament spoke about the days we are living in now. The days of Noah are upon us again, and what his family had to face and the challenges that surrounded them are what we all must overcome in our day as well. While there are many churches feeling warm and comfortable Sunday after Sunday, there is a great flood of evil that is about to be unleashed. There is a great darkness over the horizon. We all must prepare and be prepared for the battles that are yet to come on planet earth. The people of God should not look at this warfare of the future with dismay or discouragement, because God always wins and always has a plan for His people to be victorious and triumphant.

God is raising up apostolic generals in our day to lead and equip the saints of God in a way that we have never seen done in the past. I have been given the high privilege and honor to know Angela T. Greenig, the founder of Angela Greenig Ministries International. Angela is one of those few who have an anointing to do high-level warfare in dark places. After working in the streets of Seattle, Washington for many years, ministering to the forgotten, and traveling around the world, literally pulling souls out of hell into the wonderful world of light and salvation of our Lord Jesus Christ, Angela has gained insight and knowledge of the underworld. In this book, *Satanism: The Truth Behind the Veil*, she unveils and brings to light the warfare the Church must face. Her goal is to see all the saints of God equipped and trained to advance the Kingdom of God in all the world. This book is full of real-life stories; it is deep, but it is the truth. Read it and read it again, gain fresh insight, and get equipped to run the race that is set before you.

Pastor Harold "Kimo" Alimboyoguen, Jr.
Four Winds Community Church
Tracy, California
www.fourwindscommunitychurch.org

I've worked with Angela for many years in the trash dumps of Mexico. She operates strongly in the word of knowledge and deliverance ministries. She is a true general in the Kingdom of God.

Pastor David Garza
Jesus Is The Only Way Ministries
Jtowministries.com

EPIGRAPH

And from the days of John the Baptist until now the kingdom of heaven suffers violence, and the violent take it by force
(Matthew 11:12 NKJV).

My people are destroyed for lack of knowledge
(Hosea 4:6a NKJV).

TABLE OF CONTENTS

We pray that you will be
greeted by the Holy Spirit as you
read the pages of this book. We pray that He
speaks to your heart and your spirit so that you are
inspired, educated, and empowered by
His message to you.

***

Lord, we ask that You bless this reader and his or her
family, bless their health, their home, their finances,
and all their unspoken needs, Lord,
of which You already know.
In Jesus' name.

FOREWORD

Angela Greenig (my "mother") says there are four streams through which you can discover the abundance of life: walking with God, receiving His intimate counsel, deep restoration, and spiritual warfare. Once the "eyes of your heart" are opened, you will embrace three eternal truths: things are not what they seem; this is a world at war; and you have a crucial role to play.

A battle is raging and it's a battle for the heart. Theodore Roosevelt spoke some amazing words: "It's not the critic who counts; not the man who points out how the strong man stumbles, or where the doer of deeds could have done better. The credit belongs to the man [or woman] who is actually in the arena, whose face is marred by dust and sweat and blood; who strives valiantly....who knows great enthusiasms, the great devotions; who spends himself in a worthy cause; who at the best knows in the end the triumph of high achievement, and who at worst, if he fails, at least falls while daring greatly, so that his place shall never be with those cold and timid souls who neither know victory nor defeat."

The kingdom of heaven suffers violence, and violent men [or women] *take it by force* (Matthew 11:12 NASB).

Rebekah van der Steen

REFORMATION ARMY, ARISE!

I live on the West Coast where one September day, I was outside enjoying the weather. While I was standing there, a violent wind began to blow. I experienced extreme changes from all four seasons in a matter of an hour. I really felt the Lord say that it is time for the winds of change to blow again. God is blowing and stirring the fire and wind of His people as He did in Ezekiel 37. The wind is blowing and will bring great exposure to you who was hidden…and you will be hidden no more!

God had called Elijah in a time when there was a severe drought and famine. Elijah followed God's instructions, and for a few years he was hidden in a ravine and fed by ravens. The Lord has likewise called many of us to a time of separation, and it may even feel like we are isolated and barely getting by because of drought and famine. He will still feed us, and prepare us—He never leaves us! When that season was completed for Elijah, a new assignment began. Your season will soon be over too.

Elijah was then called to Zarephath to meet a widow who would supply him with food. At the gate of the town, he met her. She was preparing the last meal for her and her son. Elijah spoke to her saying, "Go home and do as I say." The oil and flour won't dry up until there is rain in the land. Elijah gave this woman hope—the same hope that so many in the Church need right now! The gate to the town represents the door of the Church, and the widow is representative of the Church. The gate (door) is opened, maybe even broken, and the widow (Church) is waiting to eat her last meal and die. God is the Priest, the Head of His Church. You see, we shouldn't have the mindset as leaders that we are barely getting by—apostasy (sin) or leaven has driven many from the church to where it has brought famine. But listen…God is looking for reformers. And He is not just calling for men and women, but children and youth to go to the gates of our cities to reform what was.

We are to be like Elijah when the child of the widow died—to go equipped and believing God for the impossible, to lay down our lives, prostrate before the Lord, and resurrect life back into the house of the Lord. It's time for the Reformation Army to arise; it's time to transform and bring back. The word Elijah spoke to the people is still relevant today: Serve God or Baal. We must be prepared for the next few years, just like Elijah had been prepared.

The name Elijah, meaning the "The Lord is my God," represents the unshakable conviction of Elijah's life. He was sent to Ahab at a time when all the Lord's prophets were being killed and Ahab had already gone to great lengths trying to find him. God told Elijah, "Go…and I will send rain on the land" (1 Kings 18:1). In boldness and confidence of our King's voice, Elijah listened. Stop questioning the voice of the Lord. We must have confidence that we can hear Him, and we must be obedient to what He is saying. Elijah's mission was to awaken the Israelites to their apostasy, backsliding, lukewarmness, and to call them back to loyalty to the God of Israel. Elijah was not just a restorer, but a reformer who sought to reestablish covenant.

Just like the Lord sent the rain on Mt. Carmel, the rain will once again bring to the surface the seeds that have been dormant. The latter rain will come and produce double what the enemy has stolen. God calls the reformers to transform our times. Be encouraged and of good cheer for we are strong and we are not alone. Soon says the Lord, the Baal priest and prophet will be shown who has the glory and is the true carrier of the living God. Sorcery, witchcraft, and the darkness that plagues our land will soon be uprooted and cast in to the lake of fire!

We are in the 11th hour; the "11" means judgment, and God will bring justice and will redeem His people. Matthew 11:12 says the Kingdom of God suffers violence and the violent take it by force! Stand firm, friends. God is setting apart His remnant, and even though it feels as if we are standing alone, we are not. For He did not come to bring peace but a sword (see Matt. 10:34). But if we are willing to pick up our cross and follow Him (see Mark 8:34), our reward will be great (see Matt. 5:12).

Are you a reformer? Believe God for the impossible and you too, like Elijah, will shake a nation to its destiny!

INTRODUCTION

This year, 2012, is the Jewish year of 5772. God wants to restore us back to the original. Isaiah 57 shows us what is going to happen to those who practice sorcery and chase after false religions. Seventy-two (72) is a sign, and God is telling us to pay attention to the sign. As this epic battle unfolds, a sound is released from God's holy mountain. It is an ancient sound, a note released like none before and none to come. It is Yahweh. He is the Sound; He is the Shofar; and with every breath of life that is blown, the vibrations reveal the colors of His glory, which resound through time and space. The sound is really a frequency above the sound that only some will hear. In Isaiah 43, a war cry echoes throughout the world. People, get ready—Jesus is coming! As the lions *roar*, the eagles will soar!

Many, like myself, have been waiting for such a time as this. They are positioned, waiting to roar, as the eagles soar, bringing back the pure light and revelation of Jesus Christ. They watch over the land and sea, illuminating, protecting, and shielding them from above. In cadence, four horns blow from the north, east, south, and west. The sound echoes throughout the land: *"Get ready to march!"* An angelic invasion is imminent; they are ready to be released. In the monasteries of Heaven itself, the angels are—and have been—ready for this battle to ignite. Pacing the floors with great anticipation, they are waiting to hear the command. They're ready, and so we must be. The Pope has announced his "300." He has called together 300 leaders from 13 different religions in a move for peace. Here is our call for 300; it is time to arise. Remember, "300" means anointing, and God will increase His anointing as we rise up!

When you call for God's glorious Army to come forth, you must have a prayer directive as to where they will be deployed, with the vision and tenacity to finish what has been assigned to you. Darkness must be taken out at any cost. It is a cancer in the very fabric of our society, woven throughout time and space.

If we would just take the time to see and recognize the signs around us, we would know that we have the fire and wind of the Holy Spirit. He has given us His faithful ones, the ancient celestial beings, God's heavenly messengers—His angels. They carry messages to each one of us with the authority of Yahweh as they complete their assignments. He has ordained for them to help us accomplish our destiny in life. Before the earth was breathed upon and responded like a scroll unfolding its hidden treasures, they have been waiting…and now is the appointed time.

ACTIVATE: THE BATTLE IS HERE

> *May the praise of God be in their mouths and a dou-ble-edged sword in their hands, to inflict vengeance on the nations and punishment on the peoples, to bind their kings with fetters, their nobles with shackles of iron, to carry out the sentence written against them. This is the glory of all His saints. Praise the LORD (Psalm 149:6-9).*

The concept described in Psalm 149 is a weapon. Praise will defeat the enemy every time. This verse addresses two areas: worship and spiritual warfare. Our desire as we praise God must be to aggressively oppose satan's kingdom and all hostile forces of darkness until they are completely destroyed. That is where the very breath of God becomes alive in us. The Lord wants to stir the coals of fire in our hearts.

> *Lord, we hear, "Forward march!" and so we continue to battle for truth and justice; to see Your kingdom come and Your will be done on the earth as it is in Heaven. Reveal, oh Ancient of Days, the portals to the paths of righteousness*

*that will lead us to You. Allow us to walk in that resur-
rected, supernatural power and with it we will destroy the
works of the evil one. Amen.*

*To Every POW (Prisoner of War) & MIA (Missing in Action) Soldier—
Hold On... We're Coming! Help Is on the Way!*

Whether they realize it or not, many of God's children are POW's
and MIA's. They are entrenched in a spiritual battle they do not understand and find themselves lost, hopeless, and weaponless. My desire is
that we will retrieve the POW and MIA and educate them on the power
and arsenal they possess in Christ, so no further COW's (casualties of
war) will die for lack of knowledge, as spoken of in Hosea chapter 4.
The arsenal resides in these pages, and as you read your spirit will engage
with these truths.

*Consider the Battle From Earth to Heaven and Back, and the Release of the
Dark Winged Ones—the Nameless Ones.*

On August 1, 2008, during my time of prayer, I was taken through
a series of prophetic visions showing events yet to come.

> In the spirit, I was traveling through the spheres of
> the heavens. As I passed through the second heaven, I
> was drawn to look over my right shoulder. As far as the
> eye could see and in a distant time was a massive army
> of the dark winged ones. There were countless, various
> military troops and many of their warrior generals. They
> were assembled around a table where an ancient manu-
> script lay unfolded. They were strategizing for the next
> attack, which would bring on a war within the Church,
> the Body of Christ itself. Code red, I thought.
> I could see the strategists in the war room. The ar-
> mor they wore was unlike any I had ever seen before.
> Their weapons didn't make sense to me at the time. They

planned an assault to produce chaos within the world and to cause the world's leaders to fail and fall. Their main target wasn't just the government but Christians as well.

They were to come in massive numbers; but as a "sleeper cell," they had to first wait for the command from their master, satan. Their objective would be to steal, kill, destroy, and annihilate (see John 10:10). This battle would rage not only in the second heaven, but here in the first as well, on earth.

The vision continued, like a movie unfolding. But I assure you that this was not a movie.

The earth began to quake violently as though from pressure, velocity, and force, until all at once there was an explosion as the hordes of darkness were released and broke forth. They flew, covering the skies, seas, and land, like the Egyptian armies when released from Pharaoh's hands. A new world order had been awakened from its slumber.

As in a chess game, we likewise need to be in position, as the enemy is positioned all over the world, waiting to attack. What comes from Egypt will set the stage for the climax that will usher in the end of the world as we know it.

THE FINAL COUNTDOWN—THE WAR BETWEEN GOOD AND EVIL

The dark winged ones are mutating at a rate faster than the speed of light. Why? Because their main objective is to take out *the Light*. The Light, my friend, resides in you and me. When satan comes in, he targets the vulnerable areas within our lives. He will always go after the weakest link. He looks for the most vulnerable areas within us or within our loved ones. Believe and understand that these weak areas in our lives are what propel us into our destinies as they require us to rely fully on Christ to be our strength in weakness. If we do not choose to apply Kingdom tactics to our lives, satan will unrelentingly persevere with a most diabolical force. The assignment and main objective of the dark winged ones is to kill the Christ within us. Satan will attempt to accomplish this either all at once or a little at a time.

God's armies both here on earth and in Heaven are massive. He is God, and He needs us active in battle now. We are His voice to His people. Righteousness must be our banner like never before. Our mandate is holiness unto our King; we cannot continue to bring blind, maimed sacrifices unto God. Joshua made a decision during a similar time of crisis when he said, *"Choose you this day whom ye will serve."* Let's say it together: *"As for me and my house, we will serve the LORD"* (Josh. 24:15 KJV). This is our declaration. There is no turning back.

So blow, Lord, blow upon this valley of dry bones; we speak life!

It really is all about holiness. Even now, I see a valley stretched out as far as the eye can see. I hear the Lord saying, "Holiness will rain down onto the valley, and I speak LIFE to these dry bones; those dreams that have dried up in you will live. They will LIVE and you will come alive, full of life, joy, and a renewed faith in Me that will bring hope to a lost and dying world."

Right now, across the Body of Christ globally, we are at a major crossroads. We need the Holy Spirit, and the gift of discernment must be the arrow that pierces through our souls. We can *"walk through the valley of the shadow of death"* (Ps. 23:4 KJV) and come out on the other side unscathed! God's love will comfort us; He will never leave us or forsake us (see Heb. 13:5). I pray He will continue to breathe fresh fire and revelation upon us all!

May the praise of God be in their mouths and a double-edged sword in their hands (Psalm 149:6).

CHAPTER 1

THE QUEST BEGINS

Let's discover and uncover the truth about the devil, satan himself.

In the beginning God created the heavens and the earth.
Now the earth was formless and empty, darkness was over
the surface of the deep, and the Spirit of God was hovering
over the waters (Genesis 1:1-2).

("Darkness" here is thought to be referring to demonic activity.)

In some religions and traditions, the following titles identify separate demons; others recognize these names as guises of the devil. Even when they are thought of as individual demons, they are often considered to be under the direct control of the devil. The first list includes names of demons that can also be relegated to the devil.

Abaddon, Abbadon (Hebrew אבדון Avaddon): "eternal destruction"

Baphomet: a demon supposedly worshiped by the Knights of Templar

Beelzebub (Hebrew בעל זבוב ba'al zevuv): Master or Lord of the Flies

Belial, Beliar, Bheliar: "without master"; "despicableness of
    the earth"; "lord of pride"
Mastema: a devil in the *Book of Jubilees*
Mephistopheles, Mephisto (Greek): "he who avoids the light"
Samiel, Sammael (Hebrew): "poison of God"

The following are titles that almost always refer to the devil himself:
    666 or 616, the number of the beast
    Angra Mainyu, Ahriman: "malign spirit"; "unholy spirit"
    Antichrist: in Christianity, the coming of the devil to the
        mortal world
    der Leibhaftige (German): "he himself"
    Diabolus, Diavolus (Greek): "downward flowing"
    Iblis: the devil in Islam; "he that causes despair"
    Lord of the underworld; lord of hell; lord of this world
    Lucifer: "the morning star"; "bringer of light"; "illuminator";
        often believed to be satan's name before he fell

THE ELEVENTH HOUR

The present war that is occurring in the natural is also deeply rooted
in the spirit. It seems the patterns of the past are coming around full
circle. God is a God of precepts and patterns, times and seasons. Such
is the circle of life.

Iran (Persia), Afghanistan, and Pakistan—all of which are to the
East—are gates that have been closed since times past, but the winds
will soon blow across the land, and an ancient spirit will come like lo-
custs to wheat, devouring. These ancient powers have been waiting to
be released. We need to keep our eyes on these sites in the coming years.
They compose a gate that will open and unleash a great force, helping to
set up end-time events.

To this day, 9/11 bears a dramatic witness not only to Americans but to the world. Since 9/11, America's borders and its very existence have been changed forever. With the attack crept in spiritual and moral decay. It is clear that a spirit of unbelief and criticism has settled on the majority of people. Could history be repeating itself? Have subsequent events been triggered by this tragedy? Could the antichrist be waiting to take his rightful seat of authority? The hordes of darkness are waiting to finish their work. Could the four horsemen of the Book of Revelation be riding soon?

We have been warned over and over again as watchmen and gatekeepers, yet we have allowed our walls of protection (religion and government) to crumble and fall down. I believe that a universal awareness is taking place in people of all personal beliefs and religions. The warning is going forth now, like sound waves echoing and multiplying, on its path to the nations.

Is it possible that the war between Russia and Jordan in August of 2008 brought us closer to the third and final war? The bear, which represents Russia, has awakened from his slumber. Could the sands of time be running out? Is the cosmic clock winding down? Get ready—the end of this age is coming. In the next few years, we will see the new Babylon in Iran rebuilt. The appearing of the antichrist (who we know is alive because of the signs) and the New World Order are right around the corner.

I truly believe that we are in the eleventh hour. The number 11 signifies judgment. When broken down in the Greek, the word means "deliverance." Judgment and deliverance must come in this next hour. The year 2012 (12 means "governmental authority") will bring cataclysmic changes in government, economics, and war. We see the signs every day. We watch world events unfold, and we can't get away from the world news. The headlines cover the globe. Yet the Kingdom of Heaven is ours today if we would partner with the Holy Spirit, obey, watch, and pray. This is the hour of the rebuilding of the Holy Temple, which signifies holiness unto the Lamb of God, reverence, righteousness, and honoring the priest in the house of the Lord.

We must go back in time and reclaim our rightful inheritance. In order to go forward, we must go back to the original blueprint of God to know who we are and where we came from. We have a living legacy to inherit (see Eph. 1:17-23 KJV).

THE SCROLLS—OUR INHERITANCE

The Dead Sea Scrolls are ancient manuscripts known by some as "the greatest manuscript discovery of modern times." They include books of the Torah (which forms the Christian Old Testament) and non-biblical texts dating from 100 BC to AD 68. The scrolls are records of events, created and recorded by scribes of the day. They are a thousand years older than the oldest Hebrew (Masoretic) text of the Torah. The English version of the Old Testament is based on this version of the Torah.

The scrolls are believed to have been written during one of the most important periods of the Jewish people, on the eve of Christianity. They provide an enormously valuable resource for the study of biblical texts and the people who wrote them, as well as of Jewish history during the 4th century BC. The scrolls shed new light on the foundations of Christianity and the influence of Judaism on the Christian faith. (See reference: *Pagan's Path* at the conclusion of this book.)

The first scrolls were found between 1947 and 1956. The account of this historic discovery has changed over the years, but what was discovered has catapulted many of us into a richer, deeper relationship with Christ. This is our inheritance. It is our history; it is the family tree that strengthens you and me. The seven scrolls found in the first cave were the most important. There were two scrolls of the Book of Isaiah, one complete, the other incomplete. We will discuss two of the numerous scrolls that were discovered.

The Manual of Discipline

Also called the Rule of the Community, this scroll gives detailed information on all matters concerning a Jewish sect who lived an ascetic communal life on the shores of the Dead Sea. This sect is believed by most scholars to have been the Essences. There were, however, two other sects in Judaism at the time: the Sadducees and the Pharisees. Each sect did refer to itself as the "Sons of Light."

The War of the Sons of Light Against the Sons of Darkness

The second script discusses the coming victory over the "Sons of Darkness." *The Commentary on the Book of Habakkuk* tells of the defiling of the Sanctuary of God and the persecution of the Teacher of Righteousness, who was driven into exile by the Wicked Priest.1

The epic battle continues…as it has ever since the original choice to rebel. Our enemy is still the same. We are fighting against a great darkness that has consumed many of God's children. Sometimes we have no fear of God because we know He is a God of love and mercy. We think very little of holiness and righteousness because we have traded these for lawlessness and debauchery. The Bible, which includes the Law and the Ten Commandments, consists of God's mandates for our lives.

The information you will receive from reading this book will confirm that there is a hierarchy. In the natural, on earth, we have presidents, queens, kings, and governments with many levels and chains of command. We will unfold and bring truth concerning angels and demons, including the fact that they possess an elaborate infrastructure.

As we learn, and as we watch and pray, we are more equipped to understand the signs. This is warfare, and we must respond to God's military commands. He has already given us preparatory commands, such as "In cadence," "Forward," and "Double-time." These prepare us for the command of execution: "March!" We are to know what to expect because of what has already been done, and to know what to listen for because of what we have heard and have been told by Him and in His Word.

ISRAEL AND THE COMING UPHEAVAL

The world has kept its eyes on Israel. Right now, there are terrorists living and working throughout America who are anti-Semitic. At the time of this writing, on the world news in Florida, there were many stories about Muslims picketing and rioting, hoping to destroy Gaza. Since then an annual report by the Coordination Forum for Countering Anti-Semitism found that incidents of anti-Semitism have increased dramatically in recent years, particularly in Western Europe.[2]

On December 27, 2008, Israel began "Operation Cast Lead" to stop Iran-backed Hamas in Gaza from continuing its decade-long campaign of attacking Israeli civilians with thousands of rockets, missiles, and mortars. Following are facts and figures released by the IDF and related to Israel's decision to launch "Operation Cast Lead":

> 9,400+ rockets and mortars fired from Gaza since 2003.
>
> 3,200+ rockets and mortars fired from Gaza in 2008.
>
> 7,000+ rockets and mortars fired from Gaza since Israel withdrew from Gaza in 2005.
>
> 543+ rockets and mortars fired…during the ceasefire from June 19 to December 19, 2008.
>
> 28 deaths caused by rockets and mortars fired from Gaza into Israel since 2001.
>
> 1,000+ people in Israel injured from rockets and mortars fired from Gaza since 2001.[3]

We have to take a stand now. We have a mandate from Heaven that echoes throughout eternity. Yahweh has said that we are to protect the great nation of Israel. Our destiny is to partner with Israel, and this must be fulfilled at all costs.

If you were to look at a map of the United States from the East Coast westward, you would see the likeness of the Tabernacle of the

Lord, from the outer court into the inner court and from the inner court to the Holy of Holies. The U.S. is laid out in the shape of the Tabernacle, a prophetic sign that it is ordained by God Himself that we stand with Israel, where the Tabernacle itself once stood. We must be mindful of this sovereign assignment.

We are messengers of God to the world. And true to our motto, "United we stand; divided we fall," the United States must not compromise its assignment and mandate to stand with the nation of Israel.

Satan does his best work by using his foot soldiers. In Ephesians 6:12, the Word declares, *"For we wrestle not against flesh and blood, but against principalities, against powers, against the rulers of the darkness of this world, against spiritual wickedness in high places"* (KJV). Nations and individuals are possessed by these entities, as are the regions in which people live and even their generational and ethnic heritages, which influence who they are and where they live. As always, we can choose life or death, as God has given us the choice to make. We must choose to take a stand and break off the powers of the enemy over our lives, our families, our friends, and our nations in the Mighty Name of Jesus!

A PROPHETIC TIMELINE

History records that war often surrounds the time frame of the month of Av in the Jewish calendar. Why?

To answer this question, we must consider the building and destruction of both Temples in Jerusalem. According to the Hebrew Bible, the First Temple was built by King Solomon (reigned c 970-c 930). There are three important facts to first recognize. 1) The Temple was the center of ancient Judaism according to Hebrew scripture. 2) As the sole place of Jewish sacrifice, the Temple replaced the local sanctuaries and crude altars in the hills. 3) This First Temple was destroyed by the Babylonians in 587 BCE when they sacked the city. Construction of a new temple began in 537 BCE; after a hiatus, work resumed 520 BCE, with completion occurring in 516 BCE and dedication in 515. According to the Book of Ezra, rebuilding of the Temple was authorized by Cyrus the Great and ratified by Darius the Great. Five centuries later, this Second Temple was renovated by Herod the Great in about 20 BCE, also known as Herod's Temple. It was subsequently destroyed by the Romans in 70 CE (see "The Siege of Jerusalem in 70 CE"). All of the outer walls still stand today, although the Temple itself has long since been destroyed, and for many years it was believed that the western wall of the complex was the only wall standing.

This Western Wall is sometimes called the Ancient Gateway. It is said that both Temples were destroyed during the month of Av. Thus, this month has always been a time of mourning as well as a time of sincere repentance.

There is much controversy regarding who owns the land surrounding the Temple—the Palestinians or the Jews. As Christians, we know that our Jewish brothers and sisters are the rightful heirs to this land and to the Temple Mount. Prophecies about this land will reveal much more in the next few years.

PAKISTAN IS A KEY TO THE CHALLENGES AHEAD

Get ready, for we are living in a time where a great unleashing of darkness has entered through the gates of Iran (Persia), Afghanistan, and Pakistan. This darkness will spread around the world. We will witness an evil—an unprecedented magnitude of darkness—that we have never before dealt with. The assignment? Total annihilation. Even so, we have weapons of mass destruction in our mouths as we declare the words of the living God. Truth and justice will turn back the darkness.

I was in Lahore, Pakistan in March of 2007, along with my spiritual son. We were conducting a massive crusade in the center of the city. As I began to teach on the Temple of God, I was given an amazing vision. While I was standing onstage, I was so caught up in the glory that I immediately conveyed a revelation as to what would take place in 2008 and what would come thereafter. I saw three arches that represented 2009, 2010, and 2011. The Lord said, "Daughter, it's 9-11 or 9 through 11." He was referring to a three-year window ('09-'11) that will bring cataclysmic events, resembling the events in the U.S. on 9/11 in magnitude.

That night, a bishop had to pick me up off the platform and help me to my seat. I was lying prostrate and could not get up. The anointing, the glory, and the presence of God were so strong that I could barely breathe. I was professing what I had seen and what was to come. The next day, I saw a picture of a corridor with three archways in the newspapers, exactly as I had seen and described it the night before. The headline announced, "These are the challenges we are facing."

Pakistan is a key to end-time events. I'm so blessed to have many wonderful family members and super friends there. I love that great nation—and all of God's children—Muslim and Christian alike. Love is the greatest key in our arsenal to prevail against the warfare of this world. Love shatters stereotypes, unites religions and denominations, and breaks down even the mightiest walls—and no love is greater than the love of Christ.

Famines, Plagues, and Natural Disasters

We have experienced and continue to experience major problems in the world's economy, including a plunge in the stock market. Entire regions have experienced significant reductions in their exports, which were once used to help feed the world, but are now crippled. Banks have gone bankrupt and have needed assistance from the federal government to bail them out. We've seen catastrophic changes in the U.S., which has affected the economy of the world. Those of us who know our God have nothing to fear. Throughout history, wars and rumors of wars, earthquakes, and famine have been part of the journey of life. The key is whom you walk with—God the Father of faith, or satan the father of fear.

Ten to twenty years ago, earthquakes were occurring sporadically from Pakistan to the state of Washington. Today, there is an increase in wars, rumors of wars, and natural disasters such as earthquakes, tsunamis, pestilence, droughts, and famines. In Africa, 2008 was a year like none before (and hopefully none to come) regarding malaria. Medicine that had worked in 2007 stopped working. Disasters like this are drastically affecting the world and the market. Sometimes this is referred to as the "chaos theory," and it appears that the earth itself is in travail. The earth yearns for the Creator, God Himself.

WE MUST FIGHT WITH THE WEAPONS OF TRUTH

In order to face the impending crises and natural disasters, we must operate in the opposite spirit and fight back both in the natural and spiritual realms. Even in the midst of this epic battle, mankind truly desires peace and *freedom*—to be released and rescued from physical oppression, and to gain the right to speak and act without restriction, interference, bondage, or fear of being confined, enslaved, captured, or imprisoned. Yet freedom will always cost you something. In fact, I always say that freedom will cost you everything! Still, there is no price too high to pay for it.

This journey we are about to take will be like breaking through the earth's crust; there are many layers that we will dig and sift through in order to bring forth full revelation. So, in order to prepare you for this great, end-time global drama, I want to offer you spiritual keys that can save you decades of time in the natural. I want to walk you through some gates that you might never have entered before. So let's pray:

Holy Spirit, we ask You to open up our understanding, just like the Western Gate opens up times past. Lord, we

pray for wisdom, power, and a sound, strong mind that
helps us to discern and understand the seasons we are in.
May Your wisdom rest upon us, Lord. Amen.

These are the last days. This truly is the final countdown before Jesus Christ comes back. These are very uncertain but exciting times in history, as prophecy is being fulfilled at an accelerated rate.

This is the time for *Satanism: The Truth Behind the Veil*. I began writing this book during the season of Tisha B'Av, the annual fast day in Judaism, named for the ninth day (Tisha) of the month of Av in the Hebrew calendar. The fast commemorates the destruction of the first and second Temples in Jerusalem, events that occurred 656 years apart—on the same date. Accordingly, the day has been called "the saddest day in Jewish history."

What I believe, and know, is that on August 1, 2008, there was another unleashing of high and satanic proportion. Those of you who have studied warfare will understand the statement I'm about to make: In order to be able to take out this higher level of the demonic forces, we must have the proper weapons. After all, they have diabolical schemes and weapons! Satan has been plotting since his first rebellion, when he desired to be God.

I have been praying and asking the Lord to raise up and send out His Army. We are experiencing Isaiah 11:11. The weapons that we are fighting with right now are not adequate in defeating the enemy. This dark force that has invaded the land can be slowed down, but cannot yet be fully taken out. I want to use the weapons God has given us to take out the dark, winged ones for good! As Christians who have the Truth, we will march forward. We will not turn back. And satan and his armies will be destroyed.

CHAPTER 2

WE ARE EQUIPPED

Now the glory of the God of Israel went up from above the cherubim, where it had been, and moved to the threshold of the temple. Then the LORD called to the man clothed in linen who had the writing kit at his side and said to him, "Go throughout the city of Jerusalem and put a mark on the foreheads of those who grieve and lament over all the detestable things that are done in it" (Ezekiel 9:3-4).

The cherubim, as referred to in the Scripture above, are intercessors who operate in a strong anointing of revelatory knowledge. In this hour, we need intercession and we need revelation from Heaven like never before. The Bible offers us the promise that, when we call out and command the angels, Heaven responds.

The LORD has established His throne in heaven, and His kingdom rules over all. Praise the LORD, you His angels, you mighty ones who do His bidding, who obey His word (Psalm 103:19-20).

In the previous chapter, we mentioned the Jewish Temples that were built on Mount Moriah. And do you know that Jacob wrestled with the angel of the Lord where the Temples were later built (see Gen. 32:24-30)? This physical location possesses an open Heaven. It is an ancient portal or what many call "Jacob's ladder."

> *He had a dream in which he saw a stairway resting on the earth, with its top reaching to heaven, and the angels of God were ascending and descending on it* (Genesis 28:12).

It is important for us to understand not only the season we are in but what the Holy Bible is telling us. Hosea 4:6a implies that we need to ask the Holy Spirit for the discerning of spirits; otherwise, we will perish for lack of knowledge and understanding: "*My people are destroyed from lack of knowledge. Because you have rejected knowledge, I also reject you as My priests.*"

As the Holy Spirit increases our understanding, we will be able to step into new territories, just like Joshua did. God is calling His Body to cross over the Jordan, to possess new ground, and to inherit the Promised Land. It comes with a price, though. There will always be causalities of war, but we will cross over and make every effort to lose none. As we are faithful in the small things, God will increase our gifts, and we will take the nations as our inheritance and the ends of the earth as our possession (see Luke 16:10).

> *Ask of Me, and I will make the nations your inheritance, the ends of the earth your possession* (Psalm 2:8).

But if we are not faithful over towns or cities (the small things), how can we expect to take the nations? Yet Matthew 28 commands us to disciple nations.

> *Therefore go and make disciples of all nations, baptizing them in the name of the Father and of the Son and of the Holy Spirit* (Matthew 28:19).

And whenever we gain new ground, we face greater warfare. As the saying goes, "Greater levels, greater devils." Therefore, as we climb higher, we must be armed with greater weapons to war against a more intense onslaught from the enemy. We have received salvation through the blood of the Lamb and the perfect, finished work of the cross. Thus, one of our greatest tools is our Sword—His Word—as well as the gifts of the Spirit. The Lord also arms and equips us with new strategies straight from Heaven's throne as to how to accomplish the work of His Kingdom.

In the midst of war, we sometimes get battle-weary. However, the rewards of being faithful far outweigh the circumstances or problems that we encounter. It's all about souls, souls, and souls! They are waiting to have their names written in the Lamb's Book of Life. The Father waits for His children who are lost to come home.

Time is running out…get ready.

The Angelic Versus the Demonic

In my book *Basic Training*, I broke down in detail the infrastructure of angels and demons by examining key passages in the Word of God. The demonic realm operates via various levels of authority, as does the angelic realm. Let's look at Ephesians 6:12 once more: *"For our struggle is not against flesh and blood, but against the rulers, against the authorities, against the powers of this dark world and against the spiritual forces of evil in the heavenly realms."*

The hierarchy in the demonic realm is much like order of rank in the military. At the highest level are principalities, followed by powers, rulers of darkness, and spirits of wickedness, all of which are satan's officers. Demons are his foot soldiers here on earth. All levels carry out his plans in the hierarchy of his kingdom.

Notice the following hierarchy parallels:

God	vs.	satan
Holy Spirit	vs.	familiar spirit
Archangels	vs.	principalities
Seraphim	vs.	powers
Cherubim	vs.	rulers of darkness
Living Creatures	vs.	spirits of wickedness
Guardian Angels	vs.	demons

Satan's apostasy led him into the greatest conflict the universe has ever seen. Having been given the freedom to choose, many angels joined lucifer. The result—their rebellion led them to their own demise. It is written that when lucifer fell, he took one third of the angels in Heaven with him (see Rev. 12:3-4,7-9). Those angels who had followed him were cast out with him. He wanted to be God and take over the universe. He did not know God would use His only Son, Jesus, to bring order back to a chaotic world.

What are demons? Where did they come from? In Latin, the word is *daemon*, which means an evil spirit or divinity. In Greek, the word is *daimon* and means an evil spirit; a source or agent of evil, harm, distress, or ruin; or an attendant power.[4] Following are a few theories and Scriptures.

Cherubim (symbolical, winged figures of unknown form) came into man, and they became demons.

> *You were anointed as a guardian cherub, for so I ordained you. You were on the holy mount of God; you walked among the fiery stones. You were blameless in your ways from the day you were created till wickedness was found in you (Ezekiel 28:14-15).*

Demons are fallen angels (which most Bible scholars believe).

> *But when the Pharisees heard this, they said, "It is only by Beelzebub, the prince of demons, that this fellow drives out demons"* (Matthew 12:24).

> *And the angels who did not keep their positions of authority but abandoned their own home—these He has kept in darkness, bound with everlasting chains for judgment on the great Day* (Jude 6).

> *His tail swept a third of the stars out of the sky and flung them to the earth. The dragon stood in front of the woman who was about to give birth, so that he might devour her child the moment it was born. ... And there was war in heaven. Michael and his angels fought against the dragon, and the dragon and his angels fought back. ... The great dragon was hurled down—that ancient serpent called the devil, or satan, who leads the whole world astray. He was hurled to the earth, and his angels with him* (Revelation 12:4,7,9).

Demons are behind idols and false gods.

> *They sacrificed to demons, which are not God— gods they had not known, gods that recently appeared, gods your fathers did not fear* (Deuteronomy 32:17).

> *They must no longer offer any of their sacrifices to the goat idols to whom they prostitute themselves. This is to be a lasting ordinance for them and for the generations to come* (Leviticus 17:7).

> *They sacrificed their sons and their daughters to demons* (Psalm 106:37).

> *Do I mean then that food sacrificed to an idol is anything, or that an idol is anything? No, but the sacrifices*

*of pagans are offered to demons, not to God, and I do not
want you to be participants with demons. You cannot drink
the cup of the Lord and the cup of demons too; you cannot have a part in both the Lord's Table and the table of
demons. Are we trying to arouse the Lord's jealousy? Are we
stronger than He?* (1 Corinthians 10:19-22)

KNOW THE ENEMY AND KNOW YOURSELF

The Holy Spirit is inviting us on a journey throughout time. We
must know our enemy; we must understand the beliefs, nature, and operation of satan and the satanic church so that we will not come under
the influence of their evil. Many have tried to "get the better" of the
demonic realm and have been unsuccessful. Whole families have been
destroyed through lack of understanding. Many times, instead of tearing
down strongholds, people have fallen into deception. It is impossible to
wage war successfully without wisdom. We can glean this wisdom from
those who have courageously waged war against the powers of darkness
and now live to share the spoils of their victories.

In Mark chapter 11, Jesus cursed a fig tree because it bore no
fruit. Just as Jesus cursed the tree for its barrenness, we must also use the
power of our tongue to wage war and curse the works of darkness. To
begin with, we need to curse the very seeds that give rise to trouble.
Then we can destroy the works of the enemy by releasing the wind and
fire of God's very breath to rekindle the dreams and visions He has given
to His people. Freedom—*let it reign!*

Likewise, you must know yourself. If you do not remember where
you came from or know who you are today, it will be impossible for
you to step into your destiny. There is so much at stake: Souls! God's
children are waiting to come home. This is our legacy, and this is our
future. The war is here and now!

*And from the days of John the Baptist until now the
kingdom of heaven suffers violence, and the violent take it
by force* (Matthew 11:12 NKJV).

We will set our faces like flint and set our hearts on this pilgrim-
age, never looking back (see Isa. 50:7; Ps. 84:5). But first things first:
we must recognize the enemy; then we will be able to take him out.
We will reverse the curses—the assignments that have been spearheaded
against God's people, our families—and then we will release the wind
and fire of the Holy Spirit. Something I frequently find myself sharing
with people is, "Curse the seed and pull up all the weeds!" This is how
wars are won! We have the victory, and we will change the world.

It is imperative that we be careful about the seeds we choose to allow
into our lives. Whether a seed comes from the Tree of Life or the tree
of death, within that tiny seed is a whole forest. A seed of pornography
(for example, watching an immoral movie) can result in a forest (such as
a full-blown addiction to pornography) a year later. We must recognize
seeds and their source.

No general in any war has ever battled his opponent without assessing him. This is good strategy, and this is how to defeat the enemy every
time. We will defeat satan and his hierarchy, the dark kingdom, and the
underworld with knowledge gained from past victories and defeats.

Let's look at a couple points:

There are angels with weapons. Consider the following verses:

*And I saw six men coming from the direction of the
upper gate, which faces north, each with a deadly weapon
in his hand. With them was a man clothed in linen who
had a writing kit at his side. They came in and stood beside
the bronze altar. Now the glory of the God of Israel went up
from above the cherubim, where it had been, and moved to
the threshold of the temple. Then the LORD called to the*

man clothed in linen who had the writing kit at his side and said to him, "Go throughout the city of Jerusalem and put a mark on the foreheads of those who grieve and lament over all the detestable things that are done in it" (Ezekiel 9:2-4).

There is also key information in the Book of Job.

His sons used to take turns holding feasts in their homes, and they would invite their three sisters to eat and drink with them. When a period of feasting had run its course, Job would send and have them purified. Early in the morning he would sacrifice a burnt offering for each of them, thinking, "Perhaps my children have sinned and cursed God in their hearts." This was Job's regular custom.

One day the angels came to present themselves before the LORD, and satan also came with them. The LORD said to satan, "Where have you come from?"

Satan answered the LORD, "From roaming through the earth and going back and forth in it."

Then the LORD said to satan, "Have you considered my servant Job? There is no one on earth like him; he is blameless and upright, a man who fears God and shuns evil."

"Does Job fear God for nothing?" satan replied. "Have You not put a hedge around him and his household and everything he has? You have blessed the work of his hands, so that his flocks and herds are spread throughout the land. But stretch out Your hand and strike everything he has, and he will surely curse You to Your face."

The LORD said to satan, "Very well, then, everything he has is in your hands, but on the man himself do not lay a finger." Then satan went out from the presence of the LORD (Job 1:4-12).

The key here is that Job feared God. This is not to say that Job was not tempted, as he had everything stripped from him, leaving him with only a shred of life and his God. There will be times when you will feel like your entire world has caved in around you. In these times, it is vital that you recognize that the Lord is your ally and that you have to look outside of your circumstances and dive deep into His Word to see who you were created to be (more than a conqueror, blessed and highly favored of the Lord, strong and courageous, and provided for). Speak life over yourself, your family, your job, your home, your friends, your health, and your circumstances.

OUR AUTHORITY OVER LUCIFER

God created lucifer. They are not equals!

> *How art thou fallen from heaven, O lucifer, son of the morning! how art thou cut down to the ground, which didst weaken the nations!* (Isaiah 14:12 KJV)

> *Thou hast been in Eden the garden of God; every precious stone was thy covering, the sardius, topaz, and the diamond, the beryl, the onyx, and the jasper, the sapphire, the emerald, and the carbuncle, and gold: the workmanship of thy tabrets and of thy pipes was prepared in thee in the day that thou wast created. Thou art the anointed cherub that covereth; and I have set thee so: thou wast upon the holy mountain of God; thou hast walked up and down in the midst of the stones of fire. Thou wast perfect in thy ways from the day that thou wast created, till iniquity was found in thee* (Ezekiel 28:13-15 KJV).

We need to realize the authority satan has been given. So many times, we make believe he is not real or that he cannot do anything to us. This is where we must be very careful. While satan has been given an amount of authority, we must realize the greater authority that we have been provided. I encourage you to read the entire chapter of Proverbs 2, as it explains very well the importance of knowing truth and its effects on our lives by knowing it.

If you study the life of Jesus as recorded in the four Gospels of the New Testament, you'll see that He invested more than 25 percent of His earthly ministry time to healing and deliverance from the power of lucifer. This is spiritual warfare. Some read the Bible as a history book rather than an instruction manual for today. They believe that deliverance was for then, but not for now. However, since the days of Jesus, the war has intensified many times over. We cannot deny or ignore what's happening around us, as it affects the very fabric of our lives on a daily basis.

> *For by Him all things were created: things in heaven and on earth, visible and invisible, whether thrones or powers or rulers or authorities; all things were created by Him and for Him* (Colossians 1:16).

Catch this Word! There is so much more going on in the spirit than we will ever know. If we could "unzip" the natural realm, we would step into a place of angels and demons with their weapons. and realize our own authority as we speak.

We have the ability to release angels, even against demons. In Matthew 18:18, Jesus gave the Church the keys of the Kingdom of Heaven, when He said, *"Whatever you bind on earth will be bound in heaven, and whatever you loose on earth will be loosed in heaven."* This includes the releasing or "loosing" of angels. In Revelation 9:14-15a, a voice said, *"Loose the four angels which are bound…And the four angels were loosed."* Angels are meant to be loosed, and Jesus said that *we* have the power to release them. We have the keys of the Kingdom and authority over lucifer!

THE REAL VERSUS THE FAKE

I have honestly met only a handful of seers. Usually, those seers can see far more than they can typically articulate or explain, and can even determine when satan disguises himself. Consider this verse: *And no wonder, for satan himself masquerades as an angel of light"* (2 Cor. 11:14). Although satan can appear to be an angel of light, seers can discern the familiar spirit versus the Holy Spirit. Recently, I conducted a teaching in Europe, and in the nation where I was teaching, there was no term for "familiar spirit." So I prayed, "Lord, give me wisdom to help explain the difference between these two spirits." Suddenly, I was teaching with the help of of my simulated diamond wedding ring. Even though it looks real, it is not. I used the ring to teach that the Holy Spirit is like a real diamond, and the familiar spirit is like a fake one—satan "masquerades as an angel of light." You aren't aware that my simulated diamond is fake unless you have it examined by a jeweler. This also applies to the spirit; it is important that we constantly pay attention to details and weigh them against the Word of God so that we can determine what is genuine versus what is artificial.

We must discern the present-day times…

> For rulers hold no terror for those who do right, but for those who do wrong. Do you want to be free from fear of the one in authority? Then do what is right and He will commend you (Romans 13:3).

This verse in Romans speaks of doing right to be free. Please hear me in this: we all make mistakes, every single one of us. Yet God Himself calls each and every one of us by name. He knows us through and through, and loves us still. ***The place you are today does not have to dictate your tomorrow.*** If you want freedom, you can have it!

In John 14:12-15, Jesus says, *"I tell you the truth, anyone who has faith in Me will do what I have been doing. He will do even greater things than these, because I am going to the Father. And I will do whatever you ask in My name, so that the Son may bring glory to the Father. You may ask Me for anything in My name, and I will do it."* He is a good and loving Father, who longs to give you good gifts and lavish His love on you. Do you dare to look into the eyes of love and ask for the things you most desperately desire from Him? His door and His heart are open. What are you waiting for?

CHAPTER 3

THE PRINCIPALITIES AND THE POWERS

Throughout the Scriptures, each number prophetically signifies another object or event. The number "four" represents creation, the flesh, and the natural man. I believe that satan views the earth by quadrants, dividing it into four geographical areas. These areas are ruled by principalities, powers, rulers of darkness, spirits of wickedness, and demons. We will unfold both the spiritual and natural world and seek to understand how spirits of darkness operate in their world as well as in our world.

A common strategy of the enemy is to allow just enough truth into a situation so that it causes confusion, deception, and guilt, in order to make us believe we are incapacitated. People perish (dry up, lose hope) for lack of knowledge (see Hosea 4:6). However, if we as the Church will persevere into greater truth and lay hold of the Word of God, we will be able to break through. Micah 2:13 describes the God of breakthrough, who bursts open a path for us:

> *One who breaks open the way will go up before them;*
> *they will break through the gate and go out. Their King will*
> *pass through before them, the LORD at their head.*

If we will lay hold of this truth, we will be shocked and amazed at the victories we gain through Christ Jesus.

THE FOUR PRINCIPALITIES

1. *Abbadon, Abaddon*—"eternal destruction":

Job description: drug abuse or any other addictive behavior or habit; sexual perversion, e.g. homosexuality, pornography (child or adult). Today there are countless people in bondage as sex slaves. This principality runs rampant and strong in many nations.

2. *Apollyon, Appolyon*:

This principality has one objective: to lie, and twist the truth, so that many will follow false religions. In the endtimes, many will fall away, including Christians. Daniel 11:32-35 confirms this fact, but we must pray that some will be saved.

Let's read on…

> *The king will do as he pleases. He will exalt and magnify himself above every god and will say unheard-of things against the God of gods. He will be successful until the time of wrath is completed, for what has been determined must take place. He will show no regard for the gods of his fathers or for the one desired by women, nor will he regard any god, but will exalt himself above them all. Instead of them, he will honor a god of fortresses; a god unknown to his fathers he will honor with gold and silver, with precious stones and costly gifts. He will attack the mightiest fortresses with the help of a foreign god and will greatly honor those who*

acknowledge him. He will make them rulers over many people and will distribute the land at a price.

At the time of the end the king of the South will engage him in battle, and the king of the North will storm out against him with chariots and cavalry and a great fleet of ships. He will invade many countries and sweep through them like a flood. He will also invade the Beautiful Land. Many countries will fall, but Edom, Moab and the leaders of Ammon will be delivered from his hand. He will extend his power over many countries; Egypt will not escape. He will gain control of the treasures of gold and silver and all the riches of Egypt, with the Libyans and Nubians in submission. But reports from the east and the north will alarm him, and he will set out in a great rage to destroy and annihilate many. He will pitch his royal tents between the seas at the beautiful holy mountain. Yet he will come to his end, and no one will help him (Daniel 11:36-45).

The principality of appolyon is responsible for the term "the chaos theory." There was a time when we offered a Bible and a prayer to everyone who first migrated to America. But during 1962-1964, we stopped telling immigrants about our God, Jehovah. We ceased to tell them that our country was founded on godly principles. This was around the same time that prayer was also removed from our public schools! Now, more than 40 years have passed (note that "40" is the number of testing). And we don't have another 40 years to waste. We're on a time line, trying to adhere to God's plumb line, so we must fight against appolyon—which has become an evil cancer in our land. Yes, we still have time!

3. *The Beast*:

We know he will work with the antichrist, but he is also known as satan.

4. *Belial*:

This principality is also referred to as the god of this world (or planet). His objective is war and death. He is the overseer of the occult and the dark magical arts. He runs back and forth, seeking and preying upon the weak—those who feel like the outcasts of society and who subsequently seek power and/or revenge. He then draws them into the occult family.

THE POWERS

Following is a list of just a few of the powers. You will recognize many, perhaps not by name, but by the fruit they showcase. These powers carry out the plans of the principalities and their master, satan, while using both rulers of darkness and spirits of wickedness.

1. *Ashtaroth* (or earth goddess):

Represented by the moon, Ashtaroth is the overseer of paganism. It's said that she is responsible for counterfeit healings. She is normally behind manifestations witnessed by those who visit black witches, mediums, or healers.

2. *Baal*:

In Hebrew, the name is translated "lord" or "husband." As the sun god of Babylon, Baal promotes sexual immorality, drug addiction, insanity, and murder. Some still refer to him as the third eye of lucifer, or the all-seeing eye.

3. *Magog*:

Also known as the god or demon of war, this power's assignment is to bring division into nations so that war, death, and destruction will take place. Black witches also utilize this spirit, invoking it through hexes and spells (usually for a price) in order to bring a curse of harm, sickness, and yes, even murder, to a person's chosen victim.

4. *Pafmon*:

This power *"masquerades as an angel of light"* (2 Cor. 11:14). He communicates with people through water, mirrors, and crystal balls. He will pretend to be the voice of God or a loved one who has died, or whatever else a person wants him to be. When a person taps into this sphere of darkness, it will release false hope through a false prophecy or word. Pafmon is wicked, and he is especially interested in destroying the younger generation. Many young people have felt the wickedness and influence of this spirit and have been pulled through to the dark side. Torment, a fear of sleeping, and a fear of the dark are only a few side effects of yielding to this power.

5. *Beelzebub* (or Lord of the Flies):

This power attempts to control, from the spirit world, anything that flies. He attacks from the air. There has been an increase in Beelzebub's assaults; this is a key power that we need to battle and defeat in order to set captives free.

Before we move on to the next four powers, let's look again at the tragedy of 9/11 in New York as a case study—and a wake-up call to the United States. The enemy used the powers of beelzebub and chaos to release his diabolical plan. We will now break it down into practical terms.

During 9/11, satan's foot soldiers were those individuals who had been hiding out in sleeper cells and who were awakened to destroy America. The power beelzebub, who oversees airwaves, hit his target— the Twin Towers in New York City —on September 11, 2001. Or was this his true target? I believe the Lord has told me that there was an evil assignment to destroy the Pentagon, which was diverted. Some thought our enemies were seeking to dismantle the power of money, yet their primary goal was the destruction of military power. I also believe the Lord sent an angel—a messenger—to warn certain men and women who were able to minimize this diabolical plot.

On 9/11, when the planes crashed through the Twin Towers, many lives were tragically and prematurely stolen. But—to quote Charles Dickens— "It was the best of times, it was the worst of times." This terrible terrorist attack was also the backdrop of many heroic acts of courage. Amazing heroes, both men and women, emerged through the difficult circumstances, willingly giving their lives for their country. Their valiant sacrifices protected America from being crippled by even greater devastation.

The Pentagon, the headquarters of our nation, was also attacked. The purpose of the Pentagon is to protect this great nation. Indeed, we are a superpower, and the five points of the Pentagon represent the U.S. Department of Defense. Fortunately, the assault took out only one point of the Pentagon. Had the center been hit, we would have experienced greater damage, greater chaos, and more casualties.

Moreover, no one will ever forget Flight 93, as it was diverted from crashing into the White House. The passengers and members of the crew who gave their lives are world warriors.

Notice the three targets of the 9/11 attacks: the Twin Towers, which represent financial power; the White House, which represents our political strength; and the Pentagon, which represents our military strength. We must take courage in the fact that God sends His secret messengers—His angelic hosts—to those in danger, though many still wonder why God did not send His angels to protect the Twin Towers. I cannot offer you an adequate answer. His angels have specific powers, but they fulfill only the divine purposes of God.

Likewise, we must fulfill our assignment, and be both an offensive and defensive people for Jesus Christ. Let us live by this code...

> *For I am convinced that neither death nor life, neither angels nor demons, neither the present nor the future, nor any powers...will be able to separate us from the love of God that is in Christ Jesus our Lord* (Romans 8:38-39).

Nothing will separate us. Nothing.

> *If you make the Most High your dwelling—even the LORD, who is my refuge—then no harm will befall you, no disaster will come near your tent. For He will command His angels concerning you to guard you in all your ways; they will lift you up in their hands, so that you will not strike your foot against a stone. You will tread upon the lion and the cobra; you will trample the great lion and the serpent* (Psalm 91:9-13).
>
> *Sound an alarm, Lord! Gather the people!* (See Joel 2.)

Maybe you've wondered why God didn't send the angels to inform or sound a warning concerning 9/11...but He did! In the news, there were many, many reports about individuals who had an uncanny "knowing" and decided not to go to work that day. Many had strange "premonitions" and opted to stay home.

September 11th was a wake-up call to America who has traded her godly heritage to pursue mammon (wealth). It is sad that our human hearts have become so hardened that God has to shake everything that can be shaken in order to get our attention (see Heb. 12:27). *Lord, may we hear the 9/11 emergency call in the spirit!*

Let's move on now to another four powers, specific to the United States:

6. *Asmodée*:

This power's primary goal is to divide and destroy the family, which has suffered drastic breakdown.

7. *Ariton*:

This power oversees the demons and humans who are involved with the magical arts.

8. *Mammon*:

This spirit oversees demons of greed, poverty, and selfishness.

9. *Chaos*:

This power is the author of confusion.

These last four powers have been operating strongly in the United States. In the meantime, the U.S. is on the brink of major change. *"God will stretch out over Edom the measuring line of chaos and the plumb line of desolation"* (Isa. 34:11b). We will clearly see how God has been removed from our government and its decrees and realize there is an agenda to take away even more of our Christian rights. *Let it not be so, Lord! And may we make bold stances to preserve that which You have so freely given us!*

CHAPTER 4

CLAIMING OUR AUTHORITY

Many Christians operate from their soul-ish realm, meaning that they are ruled by their soul (the mind, emotions, and will) instead of reigning in their spirits. Consequently, satan has no real fear of Christians today, and he and his powers do not hesitate to command many demonic "generals" to carry out their orders of evil, not only in America and Europe, but on a global level as well. Even highly intelligent, educated men and women of God often do not know the power they have available to them through Jesus Christ. We need more than mere head knowledge; we need information that brings authority.

If you read the early Church accounts regarding the apostles or stories of modern-day men and women of God, you'll learn of specific people who have changed the face of the earth, from Harriet Tubman to Smith Wigglesworth to Dr. Martin Luther King, Jr. While all of these individuals have had a profound effect on the world, you too have been given authority and can likewise have a significant amount of impact.

The Bible says, "[They] *perceived that* [Peter and John] *were uneducated and untrained men....And they realized that they had been with Jesus*" (Acts 4:13b NKJV). You don't need a high IQ; you need Jesus—and only Jesus. And people will know you have been with Him as you carry His presence. Moreover, from the place of authority that results from intimacy with Christ, you can resist the devil, and consequently, he will have to go!

> *Jesus—may the testimony of our lives be that we have been with You.*

HOLY VESSELS

When we resist, satan flees (see James 4:7). Why? Because God has *"made us sit together in heavenly places in Christ Jesus"* (Eph. 2:6b KJV). As stated in Colossians 1:27, Christ in us is the hope of glory; and Habakkuk tells us that *"the earth will be filled with the knowledge of the glory of the LORD, as the waters cover the sea"* (Hab. 2:14). Within us is the same Spirit who walked on water, healed the sick, delivered many from demons, and yes, raised men and women from the dead. This power by which the Holy Spirit breathes life into us is resurrection power. We can win this war with the weapons God has given us. If you're submitted to Him and to His Word, then you can overcome the devil *"by the blood of the Lamb and by the word of* [your] *testimony"* (Rev. 12:11a). You are a holy vessel, and you have the power to transform lives and to set people free.

We are open vessels to the Light. I truly believe that we need to be able to shoot arrows of righteousness and destroy the enemy with as much accuracy as possible. We are the arrows, and God is the bow who catapults us where we need to go. On the other side, there are people who are open vessels to the dark; they are controlled by witches, wizards, magicians, and the like who utilize the powers of darkness.

I have never been one to stop a deliverance while casting a demon out of someone to ask, "Hey, what's your name?" or "Where did you come from?" I don't ask the person I'm praying for to go back to the time they were violated at three years old. I have never spoken to demons, even though they have, many times, spoken through those they have bound. In fact, they have spoken to me in audible voices through their victims. They are liars, so I simply command them to shut up!

Even when I'm in a major battle, for a city or nation, I need to know only what I'm up against and recognize the weapons I need to wield in order to destroy the principalities, powers, rulers of darkness, and spirits of wickedness. All weapons are provided through the Word of God. Maybe that sounds crazy, or ridiculous, or even arrogant. But it's a fact—all authority has been given to us—to the Church. Ephesians 3:10 declares that God has given the Church wisdom and gifts that are to be demonstrated throughout the world. God's eternal purpose is being released right now to His Church—His Bride. Recall that while David was still young, he did what was right in the eyes of the Lord, who in turn gave him great authority. David was trained on-the-job, and we, likewise, have access to the same training.

We are the vessels of God. He uses us and fills us with His power and great authority to release nations into freedom and into their God-given destinies, of which I've been a witness. When you allow Him to use you, all things are possible.

A TORMENTED MIND SET FREE

There are many, *many* movies that are precisely on target when referring to the dark kingdom. Their accuracy is uncanny. I'm sure this is because the familiar spirit opens up the dark side and downloads these images and sounds of wickedness that destroy the soul, luring and then drawing in many captives.

In these movies, often the influence of the power called pafmon manifests itself with water, mirrors, and in many other cunning ways. The younger generation, our young lions and lionesses, are plagued by this spirit. These dark ones come and actually pull people from the natural world into a supernatural hell. There is a portal, and yes, it is real. I believe that this is what has occurred with many who are on antidepressants or who are incarcerated or admitted to mental institutions. The world says to medicate these individuals or lock them up. As we try to understand these people and their behaviors, we might casually think, *Well, he's just depressed or mentally ill*. But if we would minister deliverance from the demonic entities that have attacked their very souls, many could return to living normal lives.

You might think this is far-fetched…it is not! A great lesson on this topic can be found in the Epistle of James. In this Book, we see that vanity, pride, and arrogance will take us and keep us in a realm of delusion and denial—be aware, pastors and leaders are not exempt.

Toward the end of this book, you will read about two people who were drawn into the dark side. Its forces would have driven them to insanity and even killed them, had they not encountered Jesus Christ who changed their lives forever. They now know how to preach and educate others to come into the light of Jesus Christ.

Unfortunately, many people get caught in the valley between light and darkness. Consider those who are tormented by schizophrenia, Often, they feel as though they are caught in a demonic trap and cannot escape the mental torment. Medicines sometimes help, though many will tell you that the medicine causes other devastating effects.

Following is one story of an individual who has been fully delivered from medication, delusion, and great darkness.

A few years ago on the streets of Seattle, my team and I were feeding the homeless. A man approached one team member. The man was so out of his mind that no one knew what to do, so they asked me if I could help. I looked at the man and saw desperation in his eyes. His soul cried out, "Help me!" even as the demons stirred themselves up and attempted to keep him imprisoned. As we prayed, a wild deliverance took place! Yes, the man was totally set free. We were told that he had been schizophrenic but never took his medicine. After he was free, he kept looking into his lighter, as if to see if he could still detect a reflection of darkness, but it was gone.

Often, those in bondage to schizophrenia are tempted to hurt, or kill, others or themselves. But on that day in the streets of Seattle, the Lord set this man free! The power and authority the Lord has given to each of us should compel us to help as many as we can. Freely you have been given—now go give it away (see Matt. 10:8)!

It's our responsibility to be filled with the wisdom and knowledge that comes through Jesus. We must be aware of the dominion and authority He has given us.

> *To Him who is able to keep you from falling and to present you before His glorious presence without fault and with great joy—to the only God our Savior be glory, majesty, power and authority, through Jesus Christ our Lord, before all ages, now and forevermore! Amen* (Jude 24-25).

God's Love and Deliverance Are Real

We have never been as inundated with the supernatural on television as we are right now. There is such a hunger in the heart of mankind for the supernatural, and the media is capitalizing on this hunger. People are actually searching for the truth and for what is real, but many are being deceived and lured into the darkness. Pray that God continues to raise up a holy media army to combat the darkness with the true Light. While some have become desensitized to the supernatural, others desire supernatural gifts and are then drawn into darkness, not fully understanding what they are looking for. Some yearn to see into the spiritual realm of angels and demons, but many aren't truly ready.

If I had just one key to give you, it would unlock this truth: You don't have to strive for the Father's love. You are a beautiful gift—God's handiwork, with God-given talents. The gifts He has given you are just as important as anyone else's. Some people are very creative, while others are prophetic. Some walk in a healing ministry. <u>No one else can replace you, so just be who you are.</u>

As Christian leaders and pastors, we must know how to counterattack problems in the spirit. Yet many leaders are so clumsy in the supernatural themselves that they have no ability to lead the flock. There are some who negate the ministry of deliverance by misquoting Scriptures. I have even met pastors who do not believe in deliverance ministry at all. One of the greatest tools of the enemy is to convince us to completely repudiate deliverance ministry. He wants us to water down the Word of God until we wonder, *If deliverance isn't real, then maybe speaking in tongues is nothing but sounds.* We know this isn't true. The gift of tongues is real—it's our heavenly language.

Then there are those whose ways are borderline abusive and who leave people crippled. This is akin to domestic violence in the church. I have met many through the years with unbelievable stories of botched deliverances at the hands of both ministers and laypersons. Some of these individuals were led to think that they were crazy. One woman told me of a pastor who, while conducting deliverance, hit her in the face with his Bible. The force of the impact knocked three of her teeth out.

This really frightens me! We wonder why many of God's people are bound, wounded, and confused, suffering from thoughts of insecurity, and believing they will never be good enough. They have heard the Word of God and believe it to be true, and yet they continue to suffer through major trauma and catastrophe in their lives. Many are crippled and want to give up.

We must be careful as leaders to discern each case, for many of God's sheep are scared and alone. They are POWs (prisoners of war), MIAs (nissing in action), or COWs (casualties of war). Every month, I travel somewhere in the world, and I see this everywhere I go: people are imprisoned, missing, wounded, fearful, and hopeless. Many leaders don't know how to deal with those who have been drawn to or remain in great darkness. Just as Jesus confronted evil spirits and delivered precious souls from them, we also are meant to be warriors of Light who fight against demons to set people free.

EVIL INFILTRATION

Spirits of darkness have a simple strategy: to lay hold of a man's soul (mind, will, and emotions) so the spirits can then operate at a higher level and render even more damage. What you yield to—whether it is your soul or body— is what you will serve. Interestingly, we read in the Book of Acts that the anointing is transferable. Paul prayed over handkerchiefs that then brought healing to people in other places. Both demon spirits and the Holy Spirit can be transferred. Satanists use this knowledge to attack their target: Christians.

Satan will always target those in positions of authority, including leaders in religion, politics, and society. Satanists desire to take over the world, so they scheme to advance and then continue up the social and political ladders of success. Likewise, there are many men and women, both young and old, who have infiltrated the church and are posing as pastors, teachers, and prophets of the Body of Christ. They are in our midst; they are not Christians, but satanists pretending to be Christians. And they are good at what they do. They sound like believers; they look like believers; and they play the part very well. But they are posers. Like spies in a camp, they infiltrate in order to gain ground, and eventually— when the timing is right—they destroy the infrastructure of a church.

Throughout the years, God has often sent our ministry team into churches to expose satanists, witches, and warlocks who are operating within the house of God. Many times, they are disguised as assistant pastors, worshipers, and Sunday school teachers. Our job has been to expose and then dispose of the darkness. It is very difficult for many pastors when they discover that some of these con artists are people who they have known for many years. Betrayal is extremely painful.

Katrina gave the members of her church an elaborate story about how she had been kidnapped, raped, tortured, and forced to have a child. The fellowship believed her sad story and wanted to protect her. The problem, however, was (and still is) that Katrina needed deep healing—and yes, deliverance. She possibly even needed medication to help her mind and body function normally once again. Instead, through her, great pride came into the house—and with it came great fear. This woman claimed God had told her that certain changes would need to happen within the church. She deceived many by giving false prophesies and warnings and by wrongly interpreting dreams. The deception was so steeped within the church that the pastors believed everything Katrina said. Eventually, though, the church was devastated, and the people were crushed. It appeared that the only one who won was Katrina. She destroyed not only the church but many lives. Individuals were confused and hurt. Some were in denial. Many unpleasant emotions surfaced during this trial. The church was cursed and finally destroyed by one woman—a witch. Her assignment was to destroy the infrastructure from within, from the pastors down. And she succeeded.

Too many times, we become entangled like a fly in the web of a spider. But in Ephesians 4:14, the Lord warns us against being *"tossed to and fro, and carried about with every wind of doctrine…whereby they lie in wait to deceive"* (KJV). There are many winds of doctrine out there. Hence, the spirit of discernment is desperately needed! The disaster in the story of Katrina could have been avoided; the church could still be standing strong if the people only had eyes to see and ears to hear. My team and I brought in the truth. In fact, many laypersons also saw the truth after we had exposed the lies that Katrina was spreading. It's been several years now since the elders called me to say, "Angela, everyone is gone. All the families in our community are devastated, and most have left. We once had a thriving church focused on family, discipline, and sending missionaries around the world. We were a community church. What happened?"

"You know what happened—the Holy Spirit versus the familiar spirit," I answered. "In this case, the familiar spirit was very good at his job. Deception veiled your eyes. Your mind was clouded because of the stories Katrina told you. Those closest to you—your own people—warned you that she was not of God, but you would not listen."

Pride—wicked pride—helped to destroy the house. Even as I write this story, my heart is heavy because there are many more being deceived by the con artist—satan. Unfortunately, those who can see and hear the truth are often ignored or shunned.

In Second Timothy 4:3, the Lord warns us to be careful because teachers will come who will tell you what your *"itching ears want to hear."* They will seduce you like Eve was seduced in the Garden. We need to be able to truly discern the times, and it is absolutely necessary to pray for the gift of the discerning of spirits.

The Spiritual Eyes of Children

There are children who are born with supernatural giftings, given by God. But rather than raise these children for the Lord, many parents choose to walk the path of darkness and train up their children in the occult, where they are identified as "crystal children." Satan handpicks these young children, who have unusual, supernatural gifts and powers, and they are groomed throughout adolescence. They continue to grow in these supernatural, dark powers and eventually become witches, warlocks, or wizards. They are possessed by a spirit of witchcraft and are under the control of a ruler of darkness. Many are raised up to be priests or even brides of satan.

Recently, an unprecedented amount of fame has come to witchcraft through the books and movies about a boy who has extraordinary powers and is marked with a sign on his forehead., He loses his magical parents, but is possessed with a gift that many others want. His name? Harry Potter. These diabolical books and films have infiltrated our society with their whimsical lies. They seemingly take their fans on a journey of "make believe" although, in reality, they are embedded with just enough truth to be dangerous. They are designed to steal innocence through potions and spells, curses and wands. They possess the power to draw millions of people of all ages into the "fairy tale." This has gone far beyond the level of white witches, goblins, or gray witches. Sadly, even many Christian parents consider the books and movies as "child's play."

But here is the truth behind the lies: black witches. These witches are greatly feared as they ascend the ranks by causing others utter misery and destruction. In the quest for power, innocent blood is shed. Innocent people are murdered as these lunatics grope for more and more power. They find human victims (often children) to sacrifice on the table—on their altars of death. They use charms, amulets, and potions, and they can make your life miserable or even curse you to death. There is nothing innocent or playful about it.

The spirit world is much different from the natural world. There is far more activity than most people realize. Accordingly, we must obtain as much information as possible about the battle plan of the enemy so we can prepare the nations of the earth for the return of the Lord. The gift of spiritual discernment is key as the Bride prepares for the imminent return of Jesus. As Christians, we are given spiritual eyes to see and ears to hear through the gift of discernment in this end-time hour.

Witches and warlocks also have spiritual eyes and are able to see into the spirit world. Many have learned to use the spheres and other realms of the supernatural and can discern more than most Christians. Why? Because they have been taught, often from childhood, to believe.

As Christians, we have prophets and seers. The prophet speaks the mind of God while under the influence of the Holy Spirit. The seer, while having a gifting similar to that of the prophet, is also able to "see." The majority of my family members are seers. Since I was a child, I have seen angels and demons; I have seen colors on and around people (referred to by many as an "aura"). Believers are to use the gifting of Christ and His resurrection power to see His Kingdom come and His will be done. We are to take full dominion of all He has given us.

satanists, including mediums, psychics, witches, and wizards, who use magic and charms to gain power, also use what they call "the third eye" to see into the spirit realm. Early Egyptian art often includes a sketch of a pyramid with an eye inside this structure. Occultist Aleister Crowley wore the symbol on his hat. It is said that the eye is located on the center of one's forehead and that those in darkness use it to "see."

SHEDDING THE BLOODY GARMENTS OF BATTLE

Many people are battle-weary, cloaked in bloody, soiled garments after a long and hard assaultand limping out of the valley of the shadow of death. Often times, instead of rejoicing because they have victoriously passed through, they are simply thankful to be alive!

Isaiah 9:5 describes the bloody garments that often shroud a person, of which many Christians have not been taught or are simply ignorant. We walk around wearing the bloody garments of past battles. In this state, the enemy can "sniff us out" like a dog with an uncanny sense of smell. It's as though we are marked in the spirit realm with a bull's-eye that our enemy can easily recognize. Demons can see and smell in the spirit realm (see Matt. 12:43-45). Many witches of high rank (including the five brides of satan) are aware of their sense of smell, and consequently, they sew bits of hair, blood, and other items into the collars of their blouses, coats, and even cloaks. They believe this deed gives them more power, transferring their evil anointing.

A good anointing, a holy anointing can be transferred as well (see Acts 19:12). I have seen countless numbers of people healed and delivered through the transfer of the anointing via the laying on of hands, prayer shawls, and other items. Incidentally, please know that it is crucial for us all to receive healing and the deliverance we need for the circumstances we have endured. We can choose to walk away from our past, no matter how painful, step into the present, and realize a successful future.

Space 'n' Time

The enemy has the ability to travel through time. Many do not understand or believe it, but witches, warlocks, and high priests can astral project throughout the world—any place, any time—if they are experienced and know how to use the powers of darkness running through their veins.

But we, too, can defy the elements by stepping into the spiritual realm. In Joshua chapter 10, an epic battle unfolded. Five kings stood against Joshua and his men. They needed a miracle. They were in a hostile and evil environment, faced with many challenges and difficulties, yet God fulfilled His plan for His people. An extraordinary miracle took place…

> On the day the LORD gave the Amorites over to Israel, Joshua said to the LORD in the presence of Israel: "O sun, stand still over Gibeon, O moon, over the Valley of Aijalon."
> So the sun stood still, and the moon stopped, till the nation avenged itself on its enemies, as it is written in the Book of Jashar. The sun stopped in the middle of the sky and delayed going down about a full day (Joshua 10:12-13).

The precise method God used to prolong the daylight is not given, but it is clear that the God who created the world and the heavenly bodies can also suspend their natural movements for His purposes (see Isa. 38:7-8). But remember, satan can mimic what God is and does, including the manipulation of time and space.

Consider a few more interesting historical facts: Joshua and his entire army completed a 30-mile walk in 48 hours. All five Amorite kings were killed. During his life, Joshua destroyed 31 enemy camps, seizing a great amount of territory for His God, Jehovah. His methods are still studied to this day. In fact, his strategy during this great victory of chapter 10 was used in World War II.

Joshua's armor was different from what was normally used during his day, as were his weapons. He wore a leather breastplate, and he and his men carried handheld sickles. His war methods were unique, and his army was highly mobile and agile. He and his men could move swiftly and the nature of their weapons was such that they could get very close to their enemies, increasing the chance of killing or crippling them with one thrust.

OUR WEAPONS ARE TO BE USED

It's such a shame that while Christians have been freely offered weapons to "stand firm" in these last days, they have not been adequately trained by the Body regarding how to use them. Our weapons—our swords—are left untouched in their sheaths. Too many Christians have abandoned their swords in a corner to collect cobwebs and dust—even while their bodies and minds are under attack. We have mighty power and we have the weapons, but unfortunately do not use them because of ignorance or fear. I believe that when many get to Heaven, they will be shocked to realize the true power of the blood that they never understood or rightly used.

If only we could understand exactly what legal ground was retrieved through the perfect work of the cross, we would not find ourselves in dire situations. Yet we continue to wear bloodied garments, detectable to the enemy, rather than robes of righteousness. These robes of righteousness which fully cover us have been provided by the blood of the Lamb. The Book of Revelation describes the victorious end-time Bride and instructs her to overcome satan *"by the blood of the Lamb and by the word of* [her] *testimony"* (Rev. 12:11). The word "revelation" means "a hidden truth revealed." Few Christians apply the blood of Christ—possibly because they aren't aware that the blood is available to them.

The armor of God is outlined in the Book of Ephesians (chapter 6). You would not dare to think of stepping outside each day without getting dressed, yet few know how to daily put on their armor.

Likewise, we cannot face the day without worship, the Word of God, and communion. We must be dressed for success—armed with mighty weapons—and dangerous.

THE TRUTH SHINES LIGHT INTO THE DARKNESS

We are familiar with the Genesis 3 story of Adam and Eve, who ate from the tree of the knowledge of good and evil. The moment that they put the fruit to their lips, they intuitively knew that they had done something wrong. Perhaps at that moment, peace left them. Perhaps at that moment, the glory of God lifted and they saw the truth even as they lost their spiritual eyes. (Seeing into the spirit is like grabbing hold of a zipper and unzipping the supernatural realm.) And from that time forth, light and darkness have fought the battle of good versus evil. Even now, human beings continue to long for the unknown, thirst for power, and desire to be gods.

But don't you see? Satan has fallen, and his time is short. His objective is to take you from God and keep you separated from Him for all eternity. There is no redemption for him, but there is a chance for those who don't yet know the love of Jesus or the power of His Kingdom. Jesus is the Lion; He can break every chain.

Our heavenly Father is the Creator of Heaven and earth who operates in great power; whereas, satan is only a father of lies. He can give you some power and convince you that you don't need God—or anyone else, for that matter. He'll lead you to believe that you are your own god. But the truth is *"pride goes before destruction, a haughty spirit before a fall"* (Prov. 16:18). So often, when life is going good, many people forget that they still need God; and in their careless neglect, a door is opened for satan to slip in. Of course, truth does arise—but oftentimes, it's too late. When the wrong door has been opened, satan takes advantage and drags many souls into the dark, bottomless pit. Without the right weapons, many end up living under the tyranny of the dark ones, and others barely get by.

There are many bound by the darkness, and they need our help. Hence, my purpose for traveling, teaching, and writing warfare materials is to help train up as many as possible while also demystifying the supernatural realm. I want to unzip the realm of the spirit and shine light into the darkness so that scales will fall off blind eyes. I want to see an army of champions arise who will see into the spirit and destroy darkness—who will overcome satan *"by the blood of the Lamb, and by the word of their testimony; and* [who love] *not their lives unto the death"* (Rev. 12:11 KJV). I want to see thousands and thousands realize that through Christ, truly all things are possible.

CHAPTER 5

THE SECRET SOCIETY
EMPIRE OF DARKNESS

For centuries, the world has known of secret societies, such as the Freemasons, and Skull and Bones.

> The term "secret society" is used to describe fraternal organizations that may have secret ceremonies, ranging from the common and innocuous (collegiate fraternities) to mythical organizations described in conspiracy theories as immensely powerful, with self-serving financial or political agendas, global reach, and often Luciferian beliefs.[5]

Note that these societies are described as organizations that often have "Luciferian beliefs."

Luciferianism can be understood best as a belief system that venerates the essential characteristics that are affixed to Lucifer.

> Luciferianism is identified by some people as an auxiliary of satanism, due to the popular identification of Lucifer with satan. Some Luciferians accept this iden-

tification or consider Lucifer as the light bearer aspect of satan, and thus could properly be called satanists. Others reject it, arguing that Lucifer is a more positive ideal than satan. They are inspired by the ancient myths of Egypt, Rome and Greece, Gnosticism and traditional Western occultism.[6]

The name "Lucifer" means "bringer of light."[7]

> [According to occultists, Lucifer is] the bringer of light; the opening of minds and the route to enlightenment. You are the light of your life; without your light the world descends into black anarchy; there are forces that wish to extinguish your light by imprisoning or brainwashing you into accepting [society's] mediocrity. No imagination, no doubt and no light: no life.

I'd like to interrupt this quote at this point to mention that satanists claim that Christians are brainwashed. But we know that Christ is Lord, and He is all-powerful. Unfortunately, many Christians don't operate in the giftings Jesus has given us. Complacency sets in, and before long, we fall away. In Luciferianism (or satanism), adherents believe that they become what they desire to become—i.e., they "make things happen."

To continue with the previous quote…

> Lucifer is enlightenment here and now on Earth, in man. Christ, salvation and redemption: the self-love that enables a creative and emotional life, are all within Lucifer. Lucifer has stolen "God's" power and reveals it to us as a new truth; that your consciousness is the light of your life.[8]

If you bring forth what is within you, what you bring forth will save you. If you do not bring forth what is within you, what you do not bring forth will destroy you. —Gnostic Gospel of Thomas[9]

We are in a critical hour, and truly what we do every day echoes in eternity. If we do nothing, nothing will ever change. These are words I live by.

Notice one more quote with regard to Luciferianism. The following is taken from *The Satanic Bible* written by Anton Szandor LaVey (specifically and otherwise known as *The Book of Lucifer* or *The Enlightenment*). This is what Anton wants you to believe…

The Roman god, Lucifer, was the bearer of light, the spirit of the air, the personification of enlightenment. In Christian mythology he became synonymous with evil, which was only to have been expected from a religion whose very existence is perpetuated by clouded definitions and bogus values! It is time to set the record straight. False moralisms and occult inaccuracies must be corrected. Entertaining as they might be, most stories and plays about Devil worship must be recognized as the obsolete absurdities they are.

It has been said, "the truth will make men free." The truth alone has never set anyone free. It is only doubt which will bring mental emancipation. Without the wonderful element of doubt, the doorway through which truth passes would be tightly shut…. For those who doubt supposed truths, this book is revelation. Then Lucifer will have risen. Now is the time for doubt![10]

LUCIFER IS FOR REAL

In our world today, much fiction has been spread concerning the devil. Throughout the years, he has morphed, sometimes through innocent means; other times, his looks, name, description, and job title have been purposefully changed in order to deceive He is often viewed as a red being with horns growing from his head and a pitchfork in his hand, almost like a mascot of a team. This is not what he looks like. In fact, he can look like anything or anyone at any time. The devil is a shape-shifter and can inhabit both people and animals. Those who created this archetypical devil knew that they had created an illusion. The pitchfork idea comes from Poseidon, the mythical god of the high seas. It represents great power. The color red refers back to the Egyptian god, Set; and the Canaanite god Ba'al had horns. Throughout the ages, man has depicted satan in various ways. But we must remember this fact: he was an angel at one time, an angel of beauty and light. Satan is not red with horns and a pitchfork! The deception has been unveiled, and its sound is being heard around the world!

Many see satan as Latin in origin. As a catholic priest says rites or performs an exorcism, he speaks Latin. Others see satan as a dragon from the Orient, or the biblical leviathan—a type of sea monster. One thing is definite: we must be able to discern the times and the spirits that appear to us. So many Christians say that they are seers—they see demons, angels, and satan himself. I personally believe we need to be very careful with our words, as a false sighting can cause great damage to the people to whom we are speaking. So many believe they have seen something supernatural, or that God has spoken to them; but was it really God? Or was it a subconscious effort on that person's part? Could it be something deeply rooted in a person's psyche that "makes" things happen that are not from God? I don't know for sure. But I do know that we must not be deceived; the devil still *prowls around like a roaring lion looking for someone to devour"* (1 Pet. 5:8b).

Many of us know the biblical history of lucifer and that he wanted God's position. We read of his subsequent expulsion from Heaven in Isaiah chapter 14. In Genesis chapter 11, we read of man's same desire for position and power, which is also the basis for many occult practices that originated thousands of years ago with the Babylonians. Pride, position, and power are also the foundation on which is formed many secret societies. Let's look at Aleister Crowley's role in one of the oldest secret societies, the Illuminati, and the birthing of a demonic movement that changed the world forever.

ONE EVIL MAN, MANY OFFSPRING

Born Edward Alexander Crowley (aka Aleister Crowley) on October 12, 1875 in Leamington Spa, England, Crowley grew to become a renowned chess player, painter, astrologer, hedonist, bisexual, drug addict, and social critic of his time. He also claimed to be a Freemason. I find this interesting, as it is clear that Crowley's intelligence, charisma, and influence gave him the ability to draw countless others into darkness with him.

Crowley experimented with and indulged in psychedelic drugs—drugs causing major mental side effects. Whenever we open the door to mind-altering drugs, that door opens many other chambers that take us to a realm where "anything goes" and nothing matters except filling the void, which causes one to fall even deeper into the dark pit. Like a domino effect, this process often begins as a fantasy and then becomes a reality.

Even though Crowley's family were devout Christians and raised him to know the truth and practice morality, it is said that his mother referred to him as "the Beast." In 1896, Crowley had his first encounter with the supernatural, and the experience would change his life forever. It would also change the world. According to *Do What Thou Wilt* by Lawrence Sutin, Crowley said of the experience: "I was awakened to the knowledge that I possessed a magical means of becoming conscious of and satisfying a part of my nature which had up to that moment concealed itself from me. It was an experience of horror and pain, combined with a certain ghostly terror, yet at the same time, it was the key to the purest and holiest spiritual ecstasy that exists."[11]

The door was fully opened when, in 1904, a demonic spirit (Aiwass) had contact with Crowley, after which Crowley soon practiced his own religious philosophy, known as Thelema.

Thelema is a Greek word meaning "will" or "intention." It is also the name of a spiritual philosophy that has become prominent over the past several hundred years. One of the earliest mentions of this philosophy occurred in the classic *Gargantua and Pantagruel* written by Francois Rabelais in 1532. The seeds of Thelema sown by Rabelais eventually came to fruition in the early part of this century when further developed by Aleister Crowley. Crowley was a poet, author, mountaineer, magician, and also a member of the occult society known as the Hermetic Order of the Golden Dawn. In 1904 Crowley entered a state of trance and wrote down *The Book of the Law* (also known as *Liber AL* and *Liber Legis*). Among other statements, this book declared: "The word of the law is Thelema" and "Do what thou wilt shall be the whole of the Law." Crowley spent the rest of his life developing the philosophy of Thelema as revealed by *The Book of the Law*. The result was a voluminous output of commentary and works relating to magick, mysticism, yoga, qabalah, and other occult subjects.

Most Thelemites hold that every person possesses a "True Will," a single overall motivation for their existence. The Law of Thelema mandates that each person follow their True Will to attain fulfillment in life and freedom from restriction of their nature. Because no two True Wills can be in real conflict (according to them "Every man and every woman is a star"), this Law also prohibits one from interfering with the True Will of any other person. The notion of absolute freedom for an individual to follow his or her True Will is a cherished one among Thelemites. This philosophy also recognizes that the main task of an individual setting out on the path of Thelema is to first discover his or her True Will, giving methods of self-exploration such as magick importance. Furthermore, every True Will is different, and because each person has a unique point of view of the universe, no one can determine the True Will for another person. Each person must arrive at the discovery for themselves.

The second essential element of the belief in Thelema is "Love is the law, love under will." Crowley's meaning of "love" is complex and is frequently sexual. Crowley's system sees the dichotomy and tension between the male and female as fundamental to existence, and sexual "magick" and metaphor form a significant part of Thelemic ritual. However, love is also discussed as the "Union of Opposites," which Crowley thought was the key to enlightenment.[12]

The Goetia: The Lesser Key of Solomon the King was also written by Aleister Crowley and translated by Samuel Liddell and MacGregor Mathers (1904). *Goetia* (Latin, "howling") is a word used to describe a class of magick which emphasizes the summoning or calling forth of lesser spirits and demons to visible appearance, with the intention of binding the spirits to perform the magician's will.[13] *The Goetia* is a translation of the *Ars Goetia*, the first section of the 17th-century grimoire (black magic manual) called *The Lesser Key of Solomon* (one of the most popular books on demonology; also known as Lemegeton).

The Goetia is based on manuscripts from the British Museum, with additions by Crowley, including the *Preliminary Invocation*, and the essay *The Initiated Interpretation of Ceremonial Magick*. It is not a faithful edition of the source manuscripts but rather a "cleaned up" edition for modern use. In his introduction, Crowley argues that the work of demonic evocation is merely a form of psychological self-exploration.[14]

CONFUSING THE TRUTH TURNS TO CHAOS

Aleister Crowley was captivated by Egyptians beliefs and pagan gods. I believe he thought he would become a god—or a king—himself. He wanted power. This is why he was drawn to King Solomon, son of King David. King Solomon was known by God and man to be one who held knowledge. Solomon was given the gift of wisdom from God so that he possessed an uncanny revelation concerning both the natural and the spiritual world. He was also a seer. God gave him insight regarding the dark winged ones, their kingdom, and how it operates. You might wonder, "Hmm…what does that look like?"

If you read First Corinthians chapter 12, you'll see that one of the manifestations of the Holy Spirit—that is, one of the gifts—is the discerning of spirits (see v. 10). If you possess this gift, you can distinguish (discern) between the angelic and the demonic. You know what is operating in the spirit realm. King Solomon had great wisdom along with understanding, but he also had the gift of discernment. This is why Aleister was so drawn to *The Lesser Key*.

Throughout time, satan has always used a beast to continue building his foundation and his "church." Notice the twisting of the lying spirit that gave rise to Aleister as well as Adolph Hitler and the atrocities he carried out—the madness and murders as he attempted to obliterate the entire Jewish race. I see a pattern: Hitler claimed to believe in God, but he wanted power. It is a dangerous combination to seek the approval of man, to want power, and to be willing to stoop to any means to get it. It's not surprising that some say that Hitler's lifelong quest was to find the spear of Longinus, which was allegedly used to pierce the side of Jesus as He hung on the cross.

I believe that Aleister Crowley had a great calling on his life for the Kingdom of Jesus Christ. However, what you yield your flesh to is what you serve; and in Crowley's case, the powers of darkness drew him and seduced him into the unknown. Subsequently, he birthed a movement that changed the world in a devastating way.

From the late 19th century to the early 20th century, Crowley was a practitioner of Theurgy (the practice of rituals and high magick). He practiced everything from astrology and Tarot card reading to astral projecting and time travel. Crowley was a drug addict, racist, and bisexual.

He led (and is still leading) many into separation from the truth and from God.

It is said that magic is fun, harmless, and innocent, like pulling a rabbit out of a hat—*presto chango*. This is a deception. Crowley defined magic as "the science and art of causing change to occur in conformity with the will."[15] He lived and practiced the black magic rituals. At the age of 11, he killed a cat. Later rumors linked him with infanticide and cannibalism. He carried with him a talisman (an object carried or worn around one's neck, used by many occult religions, but never Christianity) called Segelah, to which he applied dried semen and blood. It was intended to secure him great wealth and treasure.

You might be thinking, *Too much information!* I say, "It would have been in the 1800's, but not now." As we continue to unveil the truth about satanism, we'll encounter explicit information considering ritual abuse, murder, and other atrocities. If we don't learn to discern the times and to understand that darkness is intricately woven into society, we will never know what type of ammunition to activate in order to pull this generation out of its clutches. We must know the enemy and be aware of his tactics and battle plans.

Incidentally, there are still many today who have maintained the Order of Golden Dawn as well as Thelema. One of my friends recently met a young man who tried to impress her by asking, "Have you heard of the Order of Thelema? That's what I practice. I know you are very gifted because I can see your aura; I see colors all around you." The two got into a very deep conversation concerning God. The young man wanted her to know that he was powerful, and that night he astral projected himself into her room. The battle she endured was wicked, but Christ won.

This is only one example involving one individual and one circumstance of the great darkness that has been unleashed through Crowley. He was the father of a seed that birthed the tyranny that plagues the world today known as satanism. No wonder Crowley has been called one of the darkest, wickedest men in history.

As previously mentioned, *The Lesser Key of Solomon* gives detailed description as to how to call on and conjure up evil spirits. Look how twisted the enemy is as he counterattacks and confuses the truth of God. King Solomon was blessed with incredible gifts of revelation and knowledge. Yet Crowley and many others have used and twisted these traits, causing chaos, for their own benefit.

The word "chaos" has several different meanings. According to *The Free Online Dictionary*, the everyday meaning of the word is "a condition or place of great disorder or confusion," which is similar to the definition of "random": "having no specific pattern." Yet this is not true in the fuller sense of the word.

"A butterfly that flaps its wings can cause a hurricane on the other side of the world." This saying has been interpreted in many slightly different ways, but the meaning is always basically the same: a very small change can have huge consequences. This is very true. For example, "the Earth's atmosphere is generally considered to be an example of a chaotic system that is sensitively dependent on initial conditions," says *Science Magazine*. We are living in a chaotic system. Every day, we make choices; and every choice has a cause and an effect. Notice this theory in effect from one generation to the next. The antichrist spirit will always oppose the priestly office, causing chaos, to accomplish its own evil agenda.

I see this antichrist spirit in the Book of First Samuel, in the account of King Saul, who initially *"expelled the mediums and spiritists from the land"* (1 Sam. 28:3b). He destroyed the works of divination because God had condemned all necromancers, witches, and those who practiced the art of divination. Yet, four verses later, we read that even

Saul turned to the dark side when he *"said to his attendants, 'Find me a woman who is a medium, so I may go and inquire of her.'"*

I'm presenting this information to help you to understand the mechanism behind the empire of darkness and how it has been released, like a thread sewn throughout time, woven into the fabric of society. We can choose to do nothing about it, or we can continue to stamp out darkness by rescuing one soul at a time. Since the Fall, man has looked for the unknown, for that hidden power to tap into in order to become a world-domineering powerhouse. This same antichrist spirit existed in Cain after the fall of Adam and Eve in the Garden. Greed and selfishness caused Cain to sin by murdering his own brother, Abel, whose sacrifice to God was from a pure heart. Cain was expelled, removed, cut off—and a mark was given to him. One day, when Christ returns, there will be those who are marked for Heaven and those who are marked for hell. They will be tormented and separated from God forever.

THE SEVENTY-TWO NAMES

A few details in particular caught my eye in regard to Crowley's writings. In *The Goetia: the Lesser Key of Solomon the King*, there are instructions as to how to evoke 72 demons. Similarly, there are 72 names of God. We know, for example, that Jehovah Jireh means "God my Provider," while Jehovah Nissi means "The Lord my Banner." The 72 demon names also have meaning and purpose. The number 72 means "A Sign."

When I call out to Jehovah Shama, I know that He is my covering. King Solomon was blessed with God's covering and was bestowed with vast wisdom and knowledge and revelation, given to him by God. I believe God has given us wisdom as well so we can discern the times and seasons. We can't destroy the works of darkness without knowing the spirits that are operating. Ephesians 6:12 makes it very clear: *"Our struggle is not against flesh and blood, but against the rulers, against the authorities, against the powers of this dark world and against the spiritual forces of evil in the heavenly realms."* Demons are his foot soldiers. We are in a spiritual war. We might think the devil looks like a harmless icon and try to diminish his importance, but this is not what the Word of God states. The devil is an accuser; he hates us. But God has given us full access and the means to defeat the enemy every time.

Notice the insight and wisdom that Paul describes is available to the Body of Jesus Christ:

> *In reading this, then, you will be able to understand my insight into the mystery of Christ, which was not made known to men in other generations as it has now been revealed by the Spirit to God's holy apostles and prophets. This mystery is that through the gospel the Gentiles are heirs together with Israel, members together of one body, and sharers together in the promise in Christ Jesus. I became a servant of this gospel by the gift of God's grace given me through the working of His power. Although I am less than the least of all God's people, this grace was given me: to preach to the Gentiles the unsearchable riches of Christ, and to make plain to everyone the administration of this mystery, which for ages past was kept hidden in God, who created all things. His intent was that now, through the church, the manifold wisdom of God should be made known to the rulers and authorities in the heavenly realms, according to His eternal purpose which He accomplished in Christ Jesus our Lord. In Him and through faith in Him we may approach God with freedom and confidence* (Ephesians 3:4-12).

The anointing sets us free and also allows us to understand the times and seasons we live in.

Whenever a gate or door is opened in our lives, we must make a conscious choice whether or not to go through. Crowley went through the dark doors opened to him; consequently, throughout his life, demons operated in him and through him.

ANTON LAVEY AND THE BLACK MASS

Now let's take a look at Anton LaVey and the black mass.

LaVey was born Howard Stanton LaVey on April 11, 1930 and died on October 29, 1997. He was the founder and high priest of the church of satan. He took the seed of his predecessor, Aleister Crowley, and multiplied it. There is not much written about his childhood except that he believed in the art of magic. Interestingly, many satanists do not believe in magic; they lean more toward psychological aspects and ritual elements. But they all do acknowledge and believe in the occult and supernatural powers.

(The next few pages are very detailed and graphic. Reader discretion is advised.)

The first satanic wedding took place on April 30, 1966. This event birthed the church of satan in San Francisco, California. LaVey was known as the Black Pope, and in 1968 he wrote *The Satanic Bible*. He also authored *The Devil's Notebook, Satan Speaks!* and *The Satanic Rituals: Companion to The Satanic Bible. The Satanic Rituals* is a how-to book, a manual much like what you're reading right now, intended to educate and train. If you went to college for four years, you would leave equipped to pursue your goals and fulfill your dreams. The demonic realm also wants to teach you, but it has one goal: to draw you into the world, separating you from Christ.

In *The Satanic Bible*, Anton Szandor LaVey writes that "A usual assumption is that a satanic ceremony or service is called a black mass. A black mass is not the magical ceremony practiced by satanists. The satanist would only employ the use of a black mass as a form of psychodrama…. A black mass is essentially a parody of the religious service of the Roman Catholic Church…."[16]

On another website, I found the following accurate description of a black mass…

The Black Mass is a parody of a Roman Catholic Mass. It involves the worship of satan. Reports of the Black Mass are valid and real. Just ask those who have been involved, and they will tell you so. [Satanic ritual abuse (SRA) is not really spoken of or even written about, but many who have gone through SRA, have the same or common stories and backgrounds.]

They describe a number of rituals that generally contradict the message in a proper mass. Participants may suspend a crucifix upside down, recite traditional prayers backward, perform a mock blessing with filthy water, use a naked woman as an altar, sacrifice animals, or perform a variety of bizarre sexual acts.

[The] black mass probably originated during the Middle Ages, when some people combined Christian rituals with magic. Observers may have connected such practices with witchcraft or satanic worship. Some scholars believe that the modern image of the black mass has developed since the 1600s, when many people in Europe and the American colonies were executed as witches….[17]

What I find so interesting is that those who follow any form of darkness, from satanism to New Age, always seem to copy/counterfeit the acts of God. Just as the Catholic Church has Mass every day, so does the satanic church.

> This is the ultimate rite for a real satanist to obtain magic powers: A blasphemous Mass, where the altar is a nude woman, and the vagina is the tabernacle. If possible, a real Host stolen from a Catholic Church is placed in the vagina in the midst of reciting distorted psalms with [sensual] music and all kind of obscenities, [cursing] Jesus and honoring satan. The fake priest ends up having real sex, with the Host still in the vagina.[18]

Yes, this happens every day, all over the world. Whenever perversion occurs at this magnitude, the dark ones feed on as many innocents as they can.

THE PENTAGRAM

Along with the reality of the black mass are symbols that have significant meaning in the demonic realm. I want to spend a minute examining the figure of the pentagram and its five points. The figure represents what draws man's soul to darkness, including power, the need for control and dominion, greed, and sex. These are the keys to luring a man and his flesh into an arena from which many cannot escape once they are ensnared. From the lowest positions to those of greatest authority (including the president of the United States), men and women sometimes gain power via sinful agendas in order to control more people and build their kingdoms.

The pentagram is basically a star shape. It's a two-dimensional geometric figure that has five points. These five points symbolize the five ways that satanists claim to gain control: religion, occultism, finances, politics, and sex. The pentagram, also called the pentalpha, is also associated with the releasing of demons.

Satan's demons (foot soldiers) are able to control and sway millions of people through these avenues, via the lusts of the flesh. Power, money, and sex are the fuel. Of course, once "bitten," or ensnared, the man or woman almost always instantly recognizes the mistake they have made, as Eve immediately realized her error when she ate of the forbidden fruit from the tree of the knowledge of good and evil. However, many have fed their flesh and fallen so deep that they feel it's too late and they can never get out. Many lives are gripped by this sort of fear. It's utterly crippling to have been asleep and then to awake and realize the truth. But it's not too late! It's never too late to turn back and get help.

SYMBOLISM

> Symbolism is the language of the Mysteries….By symbols men have ever sought to communicate to each other those thoughts which transcend the limitations of language…In a single figure a symbol may both reveal and conceal, while to the ignorant the figure remains inscrutable.[19]

According to the Concise Oxford Dictionary, *symbol* can be defined as "a mark or character taken as the conventional sign of some object, idea, function, or process." The New Age movement and the occult—

which, in many ways, are one and the same—have greatly employed the use of symbolism. I find it disturbing that while the historical and contemporary "marks" of occultism can be found throughout our modern culture, we no longer recognize their spiritual significance. However, just because the average person no longer knows the meaning of occult symbols, it in no way negates their significance. The fact remains that these symbols have never lost their meaning, and occultists today still recognize their power and influence.

One prevalent symbol is the all-seeing eye (also known as the Eye of Osiris). Here it's placed in the center of the sun.

This universal symbol is easily traced back to the mystery religions of Egypt and Greece. It represents insight into the occult through spiritual illumination, inner vision, and wisdom as dispersed by the Sun deity, which is gained through initiation into its rites.

The all-seeing eye on the one-dollar bill is just one example of the use of this symbol (and yes, the context of its use on the dollar is based on the mystery religions). Note that the eye is located within the pyramid. While this is common, it is not the only form this symbol takes. At times, the eye will have light radiating from it and/or clouds surrounding it.

PAGANISM SINCE THE DAYS OF NOAH

To close this chapter, I'd like to share an interesting story of symbolism, paganism and their involvement in the lives of people of whom we have read about in the Bible.

About 2,900 years before the birth of Messiah, Noah's great grandson, Nimrod built the Tower of Babel (see Gen. 10:10; 11:1-9). The people, full of pride and power, wanted to "make a name for themselves" and build a tower that would reach God.

Nimrod married his mother Semiramis, and together, they built the Babylonian Empire which combined their pagan religion with their form of government. They worshiped the stars, sun, and the moon; and they sacrificed their babies to Molech. Noah's son Shem (who was also the uncle of Nimrod) was so angry about this, that he had Nimrod killed, and his body parts were delivered to different provinces within Babylon as a warning to those who worshipped Molech, aka satan.

Nimrod's wife/mother wanted to keep this false pagan religion alive in order to keep the money coming in. She consulted her astrologers who informed her that on December 22nd the sun is the furthest away from the earth, but on December 25th, the sun is "born again." This is known as the "winter solstice" in paganism. Semiramis became pregnant on March 25th (Easter/Ishtar), which is called the spring equinox in paganism. Exactly nine months later on December 25th, she gave birth to a son and named him Tammuz. She told the Babylonian people that Nimrod was the god of the sun, and that he had impregnated her, with the rays of the sun. She told them that Tammuz was a reincarnation of Nimrod the "sun god" and that she was the "goddess of the moon" or the "Queen of Heaven."

Today the Roman Catholic Church has officially named "Mary/ Miriam" (the mother of Yeshua) "Queen of Heaven" after this pagan fertility goddess.

Semiramis ordered the Babylonians to go into the forest and cut down a tree and decorate it with little balls (which were meant to be Nimrod's testicles) to commemorate Nimrod who was "cut down" like a tree. God abhors this practice and warned the children of Israel not to practice this pagan custom.

Likewise, we should:

Hear ye the word which the Lord [YHWH] *speaketh unto you, O house of Israel* (Jeremiah 10:1 KJV).

CHAPTER 6

THE SACRIFICE IN SERVING SATAN

Throughout history, people have made pacts with the devil, signing their names in blood, which undoubtedly stresses the seriousness of the signing. In doing so, a person gives away his or her soul. For the Bible says, *"...the blood is the life"* (Deut. 12:23a). Accordingly, satanists—and yes, other religions (e.g., the followers of Molech who sacrificed their children) as well as myths and stories about the ancient gods and vampires—are obsessed with blood, because they want a person's soul.

VAMPIRES

Throughout the years, I have met many people who believe they are vampires. We know that the stories of vampires are fiction, but let's look closer at the overall picture. Consider Dracula, a real man whose name meant "son of the devil." His story became part of European folklore—about a dead person who rises each night from a coffin, out of the grave. He sucks blood from a person so that he might live. Although this is a legend, countless movies have been made and books have been written on this subject.

Then there are vampire communities all over the world who believe that Judas Iscariot was the first vampire and that vampirism continues through his bloodline. Legend declares that the 30 pieces of silver with which he betrayed Jesus were connected to his chalice before he hung himself from an aspen tree. It is said that his soul still wanders endlessly. Hence, it is claimed that only silver bullets and a stake from an aspen tree can kill a vampire. There have been subcultures that have evolved throughout time, and we can clearly see here the antichrist spirit at work once again through the twisting of the story of Judas.

I live in Washington State. In Seattle and the surrounding areas, there are many underground vampire bars where men and women drink blood in a bar atmosphere. Many wear dark, gothic clothing and have dyed their hair black. Their faces are pale as though they have just awakened from the dead. They not only role play, they truly believe that they are real vampires. And because a vampire is a form of a demon, a person takes on the form of this entity when he or she steps into the role of a vampire.

Many of us have heard of the trilogy of movies about the vampire who fights against his own kind. He is different—a half-breed, half human and half vampire. As for these movies, I can say that the accuracy with which the underground blood bars are portrayed is uncanny.

A Vampire Invitation

A few years ago, I was approached and asked by some Romanians if I would come to Transylvania regarding a situation that involved vampires. I answered and said that the only way I could come is if we trained and equipped the Body of Christ in the art of war. I would then come and help my friends spiritually map the place while praying and fasting and assisting them in any other way that I could. We would not come, though, unless we were first well prepared.

Taking out the darkness is a process. I have learned through the years that it takes time to train up the Body to properly disarm the enemy. But when it happens, there are no words to describe witnessing the pure light penetrate the darkness and recognizing souls being released from their prisons. I also received an email invitation in 2010 to meet with a community of vampires in California. I was so excited that I ran to my husband, Larry, and said, "Wow, God is hearing the cry of my heart! He's allowing me to meet with some vampires!" My goal is this: I want everyone to hear the true Gospel of Jesus Christ. I want them to hear about the true power that comes only through the Son, Jesus, and with the help of the Holy Spirit. God declares that He wants us to witness His awesome and powerful works. Read this precious manna Scripture from His Holy Word:

> So Moses made haste and bowed his head toward the earth, and worshiped. Then he said, "If now I have found grace in Your sight, O Lord, let my Lord, I pray, go among us, even though we are a stiff-necked people; and pardon our iniquity and our sin, and take us as Your inheritance." And He said: "Behold, I make a covenant. Before all your people I will do marvels such as have not been done in all the earth, nor in any nation; and all the people among whom you are shall see the work of the LORD. For it is an awesome thing that I will do with you (Exodus 34:8-10 NKJV).

Wow, what a Word for us today.

A CHILDHOOD STOLEN—A PERSONAL STORY

While I was in my early teens, my family was in major transition. My parents had recently divorced. This was in the mid-60s, when divorce was still uncommon.

All my family members were going through difficult times. Some of us were getting high, and we started to experiment with the occult—foolishness such as Tarot card readings and making a broom walk. We weren't brought up Christian; we simply existed.

There was a season during which one of my sisters seemed more and more strange to me. One day, she came out of the bathroom with blood all over her face and hands as though she had been in some sort of accident. The blood was everywhere! As I approached, I saw that, on her forehead, was an upside-down, bloody cross. In her hand was a letter to satan, written in blood, which gave him her soul in exchange for great power. I still can see the darkness in her eyes. I didn't consider her to be a sister of mine anymore, believe me.

At this time, my mother was marrying her third husband. He was a high-ranking officer and doctor in the armed services. He was also the most dark, perverse man I have ever met to this day. Having a practitioner of the dark arts in the family was crazy enough, but then we would have even more problems to deal with when my sister acquired the power to hurt our stepfather. One day, a voodoo doll was made with my stepfather's hair, and my sister began chanting a spell. As she chanted a curse, she stabbed the doll in the back and then the foot. Every time the doll was stabbed, my stepfather screamed because the pain was so intense. After this "success," my sister's mission was to learn as much about the dark arts as she could. She climbed the ranks very quickly and soon began inducting people into her circle. She also began hanging out with a person whose grandmother was a high voodoo priestess and who taught my sister the dark arts. My stepfather didn't die from further incidents, but my sister made his life miserable. Incidentally, my stepfather was an Aleister Crowley fan.

I went through many traumatic experiences at a very tender age. At four, I was molested and violated. It escalated from there; I was violated by neighbor kids and my stepfather. I can say this firsthand: darkness comes in with such power that it draws you in. It's so sad; all my siblings and I wanted was to be left alone. We didn't want to be touched and violated. We were desperate. We did the usual things to get our mom's attention. At first we told her the truth. But she didn't believe us, so we ran away...anything to get her attention. I even attempted suicide many times, but she still didn't or couldn't see what my stepfather was doing to us.

Even back then, in the early 70's, my family was very eccentric. It was who we were. The darkness pulled us in; we were desperate for help to make our stepfather stop the horrible things he did to us, as we endured both sexual and mental torture for years. For us, it was all about obtaining power in order to exact revenge. That was then, but I'm sad to say that some of my siblings are still very messed up. Their lives are bound by a lack of forgiveness and by hatred. It takes just a seed to destroy an entire family. My heart breaks that there are many who know my story all too well. If you are one, you are probably bound by lies, fear, and heaviness...but Jesus can set you free.

We in the Body of Christ must be equipped to provide young children and adolescents the help and counseling they need. I know that in Washington State alone there are thousands of runaways who have a similar version to my story—or worse. I can't even wrap my mind around it.

Amen

After working many years with children and fighting for them to really know who Jesus Christ is, and the freedom of His love for each one of them, I've entertained this thought many times: What if someone had told me at an early age about the love of God? The answer: I would not have suffered as much trauma as a child.

I don't regret what I have gone through; as I know it has helped many others to come into the light. But the tragedy remains: when the innocence of childhood and youth is stolen, you can't get it back. I remember that I just wanted to grow up as quickly as possible and fit in—and, unfortunately, I did. This came at a high cost.

KIDNAPPING IN THE UNITED STATES

It's an epidemic, and the statistics change for the worse every month. Many young people are drawn into the occult for all kinds of reasons. If you are one of those young people, please know that there is help. Please tell someone at school (maybe a teacher or counselor) or the police. Keep talking until someone listens.

There are specific times every year during which children are abducted for sacrifice. The statistics below are to help educate you not only about the darkness of the occult and satanism, but also the darkness that has consumed the mind of man.

Take a look at these staggering statistics regarding missing children in the United States of America according to the Federal Bureau of Investigation's (FBI) National Crime Information Center (NCIC).

During 2010, 692,944 missing person records were entered into NCIC. A total of 531,928 were under the age of 18. That's 1,457 children under the age of 18 per day—that is more than one child per minute, every single day in 2010. Of these persons under age 18, 15,572 were categorized as either endangered or involuntary.[20] Many children who are abducted never return home to their families. Some of these children are stolen to be raised up in satanism, used as slaves, sex slaves, and/or slaughtered as sacrifices.

SATANISTS ARE A REAL PART OF OUR WORLD

The statistics are not make-believe, they are real. Throughout the years, many law enforcement agencies have stumbled across ritual sites. These sites are like scenes from the worst of horror films. While hidden in the deep woods or fields, satanists carry out their acts around bonfires, under a full moon, as they chant while dressed in robes, carrying daggers, and drinking elixirs from chalices. Too many bodies to count have been sacrificed after being mutilated beyond recognition.

The satanic church offers the illusion that it is simply a counter-church. The truth is, it lures people into its demonic trap through the lie that it is all about freedom of choice. However, there is absolutely no freedom in satanism. There is no ability to choose at all. It's diabolical debauchery; it's all about serving satan. Throughout the years, satanists have become less noticeable as they attempt to blend in. In fact there are many working as government officials in offices, on special task forces, and in all types of organizations and facilities...and some are employed in your own hometown. This is not to discredit those in uniform. Many of these individuals are good officers, but the fact remains there are satanists in their numbers. They have infiltrated the police force, the government, and the armed forces. This might include your banker, your neighbor, even your assistant pastor, or choir director. You might be thinking, *Angela, that's just over the edge!* But believe me, it's not.

I get incensed over the fact that occult religions are recognized as legitimate, even though the United States of America was founded on the principles of the Holy Bible and God our Father. Wicca is witchcraft; yet (I am very sad to say) in America, this group is a 501(c)(3) nonprofit organization with equal rights. Many white witches claim they are good witches. Yet there is no such thing as a "good witch." This phrase is a paradox. Again, we must understand the schemes of the enemy so that we can root out evil and allow love and righteousness to break forth in the earth.

Celebrations where witches come together are their lifelines. They draw from one another's powers. They teach and train up while imparting their demonic powers, and they release their "students" into their destinies. Notice how this parallels Christian conferences during which we build up and encourage the Body of Christ.

During these times, many demonic doors open. The witches exchange recipes that result in what they believe are blessings. These witches want you to believe that they are good and that they can bring healing to a sick loved one. They claim they can perform incantations on your land that will cause your crops to grow or help you find your soul mate. But *all* witchcraft is evil. It is *all* of the devil, and these so-called recipes are spells for casting curses on people.

Another aspect of satanism seldom discussed is the connection between blood and soul and the consequent need for signing "a pact with the devil" and "letting blood" thereafter. Blood is the most important and powerful weapon known to a Christian. The finished work on the cross of Jesus Christ, who shed His blood for the forgiveness of our sins, provides for our wonderful salvation and life. Satanists also declare the blood as an important and powerful weapon; however, as evidenced by a number of gruesome satanic ceremonies, the outcome is death and destruction. .

There are aspects of the real satanism that would horrify the pseudo-devil worshipers who like to shock by saying they belong to a satanic cult. They don't realize the horror and atrocities committed by the likes of Gilles de Rais, a 15th-century French marshal who was assigned to Joan of Arc's guard and who fought by her side. In his spare time, he practiced satanism and was known for the rape, horrendous torture, and brutal murder of several hundred children. Satanic cults are murderous and evil; they are not play-acting. No one seriously involved in a satanic cult would confess it to outsiders. According to many aspects of the occult, "…those who tell, don't know; those who know, don't tell."[21]

Satanists will lie to your face, hiding behind the tale that they don't worship the devil and that they don't capture or sacrifice children or animals. This is not true. Those who have come out of situations involving ritual abuse will tell you horror stories regarding what they have seen and endured. Children and babies are sacrificed every single day. Their hearts are brutally cut out of their chests while still beating. The satanists add certain elements, which I will not disclose, to the hearts, and then drink the combination in order to gain more power.

Satanists mirror and twist the Gospel. As I mentioned earlier in this section, they understand the *power* of blood yet neglect to embrace the *perfect* blood that heals and sets free—that is, Jesus' blood. So they shed the innocent blood of children. Satanists understand the power of innocence as well. This is why they perform certain satanic rituals on newborn babies.

Every single day in the United States, children are being kidnapped—taken from their families. Many more will lose their lives on the day called Halloween. People think Halloween is a cute children's holiday during which children and adults alike dress up. Many sport costumes that reflect those whom they emulate or admire. Others dress up as the demonic beings they have seen on the big screen or television. For dramatic purposes, Halloween is sometimes called the "night of the dead." Many don't realize that this description is more than appropriate.

MICHELLE'S TESTIMONY

Here is the story of one woman who made it out alive…

I met Michelle a few years ago. She was a shell of a woman: empty, lonely, and longing for either truth or death. Her very existence was inundated in hopelessness. Her parents were satanists, but she was not fully aware of what was influencing her, as satanism was simply their "religion." Growing up was very difficult, as she lived in a satanic compound. Her childhood was steeped in perverse sexual acts including bestiality. The physical and mental torment took an enormous toll on her during the years of ritual abuse. She became an incubator—that is, she bred children who were used during ritual sacrifices. Can you imagine living this life? Can you imagine being a sex slave, enduring the violation and violence of the act—only to feel life within your body, and then have the child taken from you at birth?

Michelle's first four children were sacrificed on a satanic altar. She was forced to watch immediately after giving birth as the priest lifted each baby, dedicated it to his master, satan, and then proceeded to cut into its tiny body and remove the heart. Why? Because taking the life of an innocent, they say, brings great power. Killing the innocent today is no different than in the days when pagans worshiped Molech. People sacrificed their children to this idol. They literally burned them to death.

One day, I will film a documentary with Michelle and others who have had similar tragic experiences. They will tell their stories and reveal the parallels in their lives. As my friend shared her life story with me, I felt deep anger for the injustice she endured. I was angry that she had been brought up in that way of life—a little child who fell through the cracks in the system and became nothing more than a sex slave.

Night after night, Michelle faced the darkness and demons that tormented her endlessly only to awaken to the same nightmare the next day. When she was in her late 20's, she was able to escape and move across the country. For years, she has not seen her family. I have had the privilege of not only leading her into the loving arms of Jesus but also of crying together with her; and through it all we have become fast friends and sisters in the Lord. Through the years, we have walked together out of the mental prison of torment and great pain. For example, there was a time during the beginning of our friendship that Michelle would go crazy whenever worship music was playing or during Holy Communion. When I say "crazy," I mean she would grab her head and scream because it reminded her of the satanic ritual abuse she suffered during black masses. No human should ever have to suffer the life she lived.

There was a deliverance that took place, the details of which would fill a book in itself. Through this deliverance as well as counseling sessions and ceaseless, bottomless love, Michelle came through her ordeal. Today she serves and loves God. She will readily testify about all that God has delivered her from. The past had scarred her mind and heart, but through the love of Jesus Christ, she is walking out of her past and stepping into her future—healed. Her greatest joy is taking Holy Communion and hearing praise music while dancing and worshipping God.

God was waiting for Michelle. He grabbed hold of her little hand; He took that little life and gave her His life. His everlasting love gave her purpose, color, and fragrance. I can't even imagine being without this hope—the true power of the blood of Jesus Christ—and His extreme love.

THE CHURCH OF SATAN STILL THRIVES

Always remember that satanists will tell you that what is said about them is not true. For example, LaVey followers claim that ever since LaVey died, the satanic church hasn't been very active and has had little impact. But we know better. LaVey died in 1997, but his legacy lives on through his children and grandchildren.

Karla LaVey (born 1952) is the daughter of Carole and Anton LaVey. She was former high priestess of the church of satan, and is current founder of the first satanic church headquartered in San Francisco since 1999, and which carries on her father's legacy. She has two half siblings, Zeena Schreck and Satan Xerxes Carnacki LaVey. In addition to having held the title of high priestess, LaVey was also a founding member of her father's church—the church of satan, which was originally named "the satanic church." LaVey was the representative for both the church and her father for approximately 40 years.[22]

I would like to bring more exposure to this organization. They would like you to believe that satanism is a mindset much like Scientology or even New Age. If that were true, however, many who have died sacrificially and senselessly would be alive today. Many victims are drawn into satanism out of a desperate desire to be loved. The almost tangible void created by insecurity and low self-esteem make them easy prey. They look to power, sex, and self-worth to help them feel as though they belong and that they matter. The majority of young people who enter the occult do so either out of defiance to their parents, because of sheer curiosity, or in order to impress their peers. Many are drawn in through television shows, movies, video games, and books that exhibit the immoral fiber of the world today. Much of the role-playing game revolves around the occult and involves blood rituals as well as blood sacrifices (some animal and yes, some human, depending on rank and level). In these shows, books, and games, the lusts of the flesh abound and the invitation is extended to fulfill all your desires and passions.

When you open your life up to the darkness, you follow your sinful nature. You will do whatever is necessary to fulfill the lusts of the flesh.

> *The acts of the sinful nature are obvious: sexual immorality, impurity and debauchery; idolatry and witchcraft; hatred, discord, jealousy, fits of rage, selfish ambition, dissensions, factions and envy; drunkenness, orgies, and the like. I warn you, as I did before, that those who live like this will not inherit the kingdom of God* (Galatians 5:19-21).

Man is born in darkness and remains there until he comes into the light and love of Jesus Christ—not into man's law or into church laws, but into God's Word and His love that brings true, lasting joy and peace.

HALLOWEEN AND OTHER SATANIC DATES

October 31 is the date that has been established for the Fall Harvest Ball. More than three thousand years ago in ancient Ireland, this occult holiday was birthed. Fortune telling, divination, games, food, and ghost stories were woven together into what is now called Halloween. (Interestingly, November 1 was declared All Saints Day.) In Virginia, during the 17th century, Halloween was an especially popular tradition, and it evolved into what many pagans practice today. Witches and covens still celebrate with these practices and incantations, though they cloak the holiday under the name "Fall Harvest," or as many witches call it, "the Harvest Ball." Yet the holiday and its rituals are demonic—even something as seemingly innocent as cutting open an apple, which is done in honor of a pagan god. They also celebrate by using the demonic, five-point structure of the pentagram.

Satan is crafty. He infiltrates society with darkness by taking light and twisting it just enough to convince Christians to let their guard down. Just as satan slightly contorted the Scriptures in the Garden to seduce Eve to fall, he still provokes mankind to compromise.

Another day with significance in the satanic world is Friday the 13th.

Friday the 13th is the thirteenth day in a month that falls on Friday, which superstition holds that it is a day of good or bad luck. In the Gregorian calendar, this day occurs at least once a year. [There are also 13 wells and 13 crystal skulls.]

According to folklorists, there is no written evidence for a «Friday the 13th» superstition before the 19th century. The earliest known documented reference in English occurs in an 1869 biography of Gioachino Rossini:

[Rossini] was surrounded to the last by admiring and affectionate friends; and if it be true that, like so many other Italians, he regarded Friday as an unlucky day, and thirteen as an unlucky number, it is remarkable that on Friday, the 13th of November, he died.

However, some folklore is passed on through oral traditions. In addition, "determining the origins of superstitions is an inexact science, at best. In fact, it's mostly guesswork." Consequently, several theories have been proposed about the origin of the Friday the 13th superstition.

One theory states that it is a modern amalgamation of two older superstitions: that thirteen is an unlucky number and that Friday is an unlucky day.[23]

The actual origin of the superstition, though, appears also to be a tale in Norse mythology. Friday is named for Frigga, the free-spirited goddess of love and fertility. When Norse and Germanic tribes converted to Christianity, Frigga was banished in shame to a mountaintop and labeled a witch. It was believed that every Friday, the spiteful goddess convened a meeting with eleven other witches, plus the devil - a gathering of thirteen - and plotted ill turns of fate for the coming week. For many centuries in Scandinavia, Friday was known as «Witches› Sabbath.[24]

Another theory about the origin of the superstition traces the event to the arrest of the legendary Knights Templar. According to one expert:

The Knights Templar were a monastic military order founded in Jerusalem in 1118 C.E., whose mission was to protect Christian pilgrims during the Crusades. Over the next two centuries, the Knights Templar became extraordinarily powerful and wealthy. Threatened by that power and eager to acquire their wealth, King Philip secretly ordered the mass arrest of all the Knights Templar in France on Friday, October 13, 1307 - Friday the 13th.

The connection between the superstition and the Knights Templar was popularized in the 2003 novel The Da Vinci Code, however, some experts think that it is relatively recent and is a modern-day invention. For example, the superstition is rarely found before the 20th century, when it became extremely common. One author, noting that references are all but nonexistent before 1907 but frequently seen thereafter, has argued that its popularity derives from the publication that year of Thomas W. Lawson's popular novel Friday, the Thirteenth, in which an unscrupulous broker takes advantage of the superstition to create a Wall Street panic on a Friday the 13th.[25]

THE UNCLEAN SPIRIT AND THE CURSE

Witches are indeed able to curse someone, inflicting that person with cancer, AIDS, other sicknesses and diseases, and even death. In many third-world nations, diseases are rampant—because of curses. Years ago, I was in Puerto Rico, teaching on healing, deliverance, warfare, and spiritual mapping with members of the Catholic church. One day as we took a walk and I was praying, we came around a corner to an open-air market. It was unlike any market I had ever seen before. At one particular store, displayed in open view, there were skulls, pentagrams, herbs, bizarre objects in jars, and vats of powders. Then I saw a cross with Jesus suspended from it and a picture of Mary...that set me back a bit! There were chicken claws hanging at all four corners of this store and a stalk of green bananas out front. (In certain nations, hanging a stalk of green bananas in front of your home is said to appease demonic entities.)

As I continued to observe, I noticed that this store had just enough Jesus pictures and crosses to draw everyone in. The whole scene, including a very large and powerful-looking voodoo priest, should have scared me, but honestly I was more in shock. I had never previously heard or seen a showcase of demonic powers in this way. There was no fear of consequence; the demonic images weren't the least bit hidden. If I had not already been in deliverance ministry, I'm sure I would have been afterwards. In any case, average tourists continued to come and go into the shop, buying souvenirs, and having little dolls specifically made—because many people believe that voodoo can't hurt anyone. Nothing could be further from the truth.

What happened that day and the warfare that broke out that night was unbelievable. My team and I had dealt with some truly wicked encounters and attacks through the years, but the thought of that night still shakes me. The voodoo priest knew me in the spirit, just as I knew him. We had an understanding in the spirit realm: you stay on your side of the road, and I'll stay on mine. The bloodline had been drawn. Even so, that same night—two doors down and across the street from where I was staying—a neighborhood family found their two-year-old son brutally murdered in the back yard. Many in the neighborhood looked at me as though it were my fault. After all, I was the visiting minister from America who had come to teach and help the church with spiritual warfare, prophecy, healing, and deliverance. Many local people thought the incident was a result of my presence.

I left the house that very night and stayed away until we boarded the plane home. The people who had invited me feared for my life but also for the lives of their family members. I, too, was concerned for my life.

Ignorance is deadly. That's why discerning the spirits is so important. We must see and separate truth. I did finish my time in that country, but I did so with a greater awareness of how satan and those who work for him can strongly counterattack. God intervened and sent legions of angels to get me home safely. I was truly blessed, for many people had been stirred in their hearts to pray for me at that time, though they didn't know why. You see, I had sent the angels and cherubim to prompt my family and intercessors to fast and pray. They heard the call to help me—and it happened!

During this time, we had an amazing breakthrough of God's Holy Spirit that is still evident today. I still go back to that time and glean from the wheat that continues to fall off the stalk. That's what learning and living in the natural and spiritual world is about.

In the United States, there are now occult stores where you can learn hexes, spells, and incantations while doing your shopping—all in one place. Ten years ago, you would have had to hunt to find such a place. As Christians, we must stand up and take back that which has been stolen from us. Why should it be legal in this nation to propagate demonic goods? Why is it that the Harry Potter books and movies have been number-one bestsellers and box office hits? Why should the United States government allow such darkness to be swept under the rug? Why aren't agencies properly reporting what is truly happening to many missing children who have been kidnapped? The truth must arise.

Think about it—if believers had listened and obeyed (from Old Testament times until now) the commands to do away with all necromancy, witchcraft, divination, idol worship, and other dark practices, we as Christians, would be armed and dangerous.

THE SIGIL OF BAPHOMET AND THE SEXUAL SPIRITS

The Sigil of Baphomet is the formal symbol of the church of satan. It dates back to the Knights Templar. It is also called the endless knot and has either a goat or ram's head within two circles. It means "the hidden ones" or "he who abides in all things." Within the two circles is written (in Hebrew letters) the word "Leviathan." It is read from the bottom up, on the right side and counterclockwise. The goat or ram's head within the pentagram is the satanic symbol called the Baphomet. This symbol is displayed over satanic altars and is worn as a sign of allegiance to satan. (Due to the graphic nature of these altars, no picture is included.)

If you researched the subject of pentagrams, you would notice that there are many different pentagram symbols. Various cults, including pythagoreans, masons, gnostics, cabalists, magicians, wiccans, and Satanists, use various versions depending upon their belief system. However, most use a five pointed star whether upright or upside down.

The names "Sammael" and "Lilith" are inscribed in the pentagram, but not always. The marriage of these two is known as the "angel satan" or the "other god." They are believed to have birthed a demonic race. Sammael (Samael or Iblis) is also called the adversary, the prince of the world, the prince of the power of the air, the poison angel, chief of the satans, prince of demons, magician, the great serpent with twelve wings that draws after him, and the angel of death. Lilith is also called bat zuge, the enemy of infants, the bride of Sammael, and the angel of prostitution.

It is believed by many scholars, rabbis, and even Christians that, on the day Adam was created, there also existed a woman whose name was Lilith. The Word of God says:

> *And God said, Let us make man in our image, after our likeness: and let them have dominion over the fish of the sea, and over the fowl of the air, and over the cattle, and over all the earth, and over every creeping thing that creepeth upon the earth. So God created man in his own*

image, in the image of God created he him; male and fe-
male created he them (Genesis 1:26-27 KJV).

Many scholars argue that Lilith was Adam's first wife. Believing that she was equal with Adam, Lilith would not submit to his authority. The story goes on to say that she flew away and would not go back to the earth to live. Three angels were assigned by God to bring her back. Lilith was given the chance to go back to Adam, but she said no. So her life was cursed—doomed to be one of endless roaming through the night. Ironically, her name means just that: "the night."

As I close this chapter, I would like to touch on one specific issue here. I know for sure that there are sexual spirits. Seducing and perverse spirits are just two types. Incubus and Succubus are two more. Incubus attacks women in their sleep, seducing and raping them. Men are also seduced and raped in the dream state. These spirits are associated with Lilith and other demonic entities. I have not only been attacked myself but have also met countless others who have been violated in their beds while both asleep and awake. They have felt as if they were gagged and physically bound.

My team and I have met and prayed for the deliverance of hundreds and hundreds of people through the years. One of the most amazing results that occur after prayer is that people say, "I don't have to be afraid of the dark or of being raped and violated anymore." After my own personal deliverance, I was totally convinced that the sexual abuse wasn't my fault.

There are also generational curses, which are passed from one generation to the next, that often result in young children being physically violated as I had been. Many with whom we've spoken came from good families who had great values. They were actively involved in the church, and they loved the Lord. They were not on drugs nor did they deal with pornography. Yet, either in their innocence or ignorance, they simply associated with the wrong people. Consequently, perverse spirits were able to transfer from one person to the next.

I must stress again that discerning the spirits is of utmost importance. We must be able to separate the truth from the lies. We must claim the true power of the Lord so that we can lead others, who have suffered such painful and horrible abuse, to the wonderful arms of Jesus, where they can find rest, and peace, and bask in His everlasting and pure love.

CHAPTER 7

DISCOVERING THE METHODS AND PLANS OF THE ADVESARY

Says Magus Peter H. Gilmore in *Satanism: The Feared Religion*:

> There is no requirement for participation in ritual activity. The techniques presented in our literature are for members to make use of as they so desire. Some satanists enjoy the social atmosphere of group ritual and seek out others for this purpose. Many satanists find their ritual activity to be very personal and prefer to remain solitary.[26]

The church of satan's high priest today is Magus Peter Gilmore, who wrote *The Satanic Scriptures*. When he was just 13, he read *The Satanic Bible*. He has described the church of satan as "the motivating philosophical force" in his life ever since.

> Gilmore feels satanists are often misunderstood or misrepresented. [He believes] LaVey's teachings are based on individualism, self-indulgence, and "eye for an

101

eye" morality, with influence from Friedrich Nietzsche and Ayn Rand; while its rituals and magic draw heavily from occultists such as Aleister Crowley. [He claims that] they do not worship—nor believe in—the Devil....[27]

However, we know there is a devil. Read the following Scripture from Revelation chapter 12.

> *And there was war in heaven. Michael and his angels fought against the dragon, and the dragon and his angels fought back. But he was not strong enough, and they lost their place in heaven. The great dragon was hurled down— that ancient serpent called the devil, or satan, who leads the whole world astray. He was hurled to the earth, and his angels with him....Therefore rejoice, you heavens and you who dwell in them! But woe to the earth and the sea, because the devil has gone down to you! He is filled with fury, because he knows that his time is short* (Revelation 12:7-9,12).

According to the article "Fallen Angel and Lucifer" at *www.vampyra. com*, after he fell from Heaven, "Lucifer was no more—he had a new name, satan (the Hebrew word for 'adversary') and his new domain was Hell. The angels who had fallen with him (based on a determination by the Fourth Lateran Council in A.D. 1215) became his Demons."

And according to "Satanism: An Interview with Church of Satan High Priest Peter Gilmore": "The word 'satan' comes from the Hebrew word for 'adversary' and originated from the Abrahamic faiths, being traditionally applied to an angel. Church of satan adherents see themselves as truth-seekers, adversaries and skeptics of the religious world around them."

In 1989, [Gilmore] and his wife Peggy Nadramia began publishing *The Black Flame*, a satanic journal, and continue to publish issues sporadically. In 2005, Gilmore provided a new introduction to LaVey's *The Satanic Bible*, and his essay on satanism was published in the *Encyclopedia of Religion and Nature*. In Germany Walpurgisnacht is a spring festival held at the end of April where witches await the arrival of spring on top of Brocken while holding wild festivities with their gods. Brocken is the highest of the Harz mountains in North Central Germany. On this night in 2007, *The Satanic Scriptures* was released, which was his newest collection of essays and writings on atheism and satanism.[28]

PERGAMUM—A GATEWAY FROM THE PAST TO THE PRESENT

To the angel of the church in Pergamum write: These are the words of Him who has the sharp, double-edged sword. I know where you live—where satan has his throne. Yet you remain true to My name. You did not renounce your faith in Me, even in the days of Antipas, My faithful witness, who was put to death in your city—where satan lives. Nevertheless, I have a few things against you: You have people there who hold to the teaching of Balaam, who taught Balak to entice the Israelites to sin by eating food sacrificed to idols and by committing sexual immorality. Likewise you also have those who hold to the teaching of the Nicolaitans. Repent therefore! Otherwise, I will soon come to you and will fight against them with the sword of My mouth. He who has an ear, let him hear what the Spirit says to the churches. To him who overcomes, I will give some of the hidden manna. I will also give him a white stone with a new name written on it, known only to him who receives it (Revelation 2:12-17).

Pergamon, Pergamum or Pérgamo (Greek: ΠΕΡΓΑΜΟΣ,) was an ancient Greek city in modern-day Turkey, in Mysia, north-western Anatolia, 16 miles from the Aegean Sea, located on a promontory on the north side of the river Caicus (modern day Bakırçay), that became the capital of the Kingdom of Pergamon during the Hellenistic period, under the Attalid dynasty, 281–133 BC….

The Great Altar of Pergamon is in the Pergamon Museum, Berlin. The base of this altar remains on the upper part of the Acropolis. It was this altar, believed dedicated to Zeus, that John of Patmos referred to as "Satan's Throne" in his Book of Revelation (Revelation 2:12-13).[29]

We need to understand that there are gates from the past that lead into the present like a revolving, open door. For example, just as the Wailing Wall in Israel is a key gateway, so also is the Altar of Pergamon, still partially intact, a gateway that just happens to be in the German museum.

God had His reasons for giving John the Revelator this incredible vision referred to in Revelation chapter 2. I'm sure people thought he was strange or even mentally crazy. But in reality, he stepped into the supernatural, and by doing so, he gained powerful wisdom and understanding.

There are 13 gates and 9 wells. We will name two gates in this chapter—Turkey and Germany. Revelation 2:13 declares what the Lord revealed to John as well as to us, the Church. He refers to the entry point of satan's throne. We now know there is a gateway or vortex, an ancient porthole that leads to the dimension of hell, home of satan and his hierarchy of fallen angels.

In 2012, I began to teach and conduct conferences on Light verse darkness. I also released a School of the Gladiators where I teach and equip God's people for spiritual warfare. Using a geographic breakdown, otherwise known as spiritual mapping, my objectives are to help bring greater understanding of how satan's army affects specific regions, examine how they affect the place we live spiritually, and learn how to pray and break open the ancient gates. In the Books of Revelation and Ezekiel, and in other places of the Bible, we can unfold a pattern. Always know that God is a God of patterns and precepts where we can uncover the truth.

At a conference on October 23, 2011, the power and fire again hit me in a certain way and I went into the realm of what I call "see and say." I saw in my spirit (looks like a video clip) and then spoke that Turkey is the number-one gate in the world. The Lord says there is a shaking going on and that it will be a sign for His people. It has begun.

A few hours after the meeting, my personal assistant Christina called me and said, "Ang, did you see that Turkey just had an earthquake? I asked, "What was the number? How violent was it?" "It was 7.2." It took me a few minutes to contain myself. You see, the number 72 means a sign. That was exactly what I had said and had seen. The shaking earthquake—the sign—the number 7.2.

Then, a few days later, on October 27, 2011 I was on my way to Sonora, California where I was to train a group on how to spot and destroy the enemy's strongholds in their home town. When I arrived, Pastor Sharron Heuton gave me some papers she had printed that morning regarding the 13 crystal skulls and how the first skull was preparing to come through the gateway of New York. There were people traveling from Manhattan in New York City across the U.S. to Los Angeles, California and stopping at several "sacred sites" to invoke energies with these crystal skulls. The Mayan Indians believe that in the year 2012, the world will end. Throughout 2012, there will be four cataclysmic events—one in each season. March 21 (3/21) is the spring equinox, June 21 (6/21) is the summer solstice, September 21 (9/21) is the autumn equinox, and

December 12, 2012 (12/12/12) is the winter solstice. During the winter solstice at 11:11 pm, they believe that the earth and sun will be in exact alignment with the center of the galaxy and will bring a special energy to the earth. In all four quarters, there will be demonic unleashings, known as the dragon consumed his tail, and there will be a crescendo in the atmosphere. They say peace and harmony will come together as millions watch and wait for this sign from the heavens.

TETRAMORPH—GOD'S REVELATION AND SATAN'S PREVERSION

Tetramorph (from Greek *tetra*, four and *morph*, shape) is a symbolic arrangement of four differing elements. The Christian tetramorph is a good example of how syncreticism occurs in religious symbolism.

The most-developed of all *foursome* or *fournesses* in religious symbolism is the Christian tetramorph of the four evangelists. It originated from the Jewish prophet Ezekiel who whilst in exile in Babylonia circa 550 BCE used the symbolism of Babylonian astrology for his own prophetic purposes. Ezekiel describes his vision in which the likeness of four living creatures came out of the midst of the fire, thus—

Their faces looked like this: Each of the four had the face of a man, and on the right side each had the face of a lion, and on the left the face of an ox; each also had the face of an eagle (Ezekiel 1:10).

Ezekiel's vision is based upon the astrology of the ancient Babylonians in which the constellations of the Zodiac (Greek for *circle of animals*) signs of Aquarius (the man/angel) Leo the Lion, Taurus the Bull and Scorpio the Eagle are represented. Known astrologically as the Fixed Cross (with the substitution of the scorpion, a creature little known outside the Mediterranean basin was early on replaced by the winged eagle).

These four animal figures are also depicted in the early Christian evangelist Saint John's book of the Apocalypse, the last book of the New Testament, the book of Revelation in which the events of the end times are revealed.[30]

Saint John alludes to Ezekiel's vision thus—

The revelation of Jesus Christ, which God gave him to show his servants what must soon take place. He made it known by sending his angel to his servant John, who testifies to everything he saw—that is, the word of God and the testimony of Jesus Christ. Blessed is the one who reads the words of this prophecy, and blessed are those who hear it and take to heart what is written in it, because the time is near.... The first living creature was like a lion, the second was like an ox, the third had a face like a man, the fourth was like a flying eagle (Revelation 1:1-3; 4:7).

This is supernatural, but it is real.

Aleister Crowley gives his interpretation of the four beasts of Tarot cards in *The Book of Thoth: Being the Equinox*: "Around him are the four beasts or Kerubs, one in each corner of the card; for these are the guardians of every shrine." And, writing about the Wheel, he says, "In the corners of the card are the four Kerubim showing the established Universe."

This was the vision of Ezekiel until satan perverted it. You can see that the Tarot cards incorporate the four creatures described in the Bible.

> The Golden Dawn deck has man with the swords and birds and sea creatures (other than fish) together for cups. This grouping of fish and fowl not only corresponds better to the biblical creation narrative, it

also fits the positioning of the creatures around certain trump cards.... Although the four creatures are pictured many times in Tarot, in the major as well as minor arcana, explanations are scarce.[31]

In truth, the key here is Ezekiel's vision and what God has given to man. The four creatures were intended to help us understand this profound revelation of God Himself.

THE THREE SPHERES OF GOOD

In regard to the operations of the spheres, there are choirs of angels who dwell therein.

> The Choirs in the second and third spheres...appear to be also united in pairs. The existence of these pairs of Orders is inferred through their etymological proximity and the apparent affinity in the description of their work-activity.[32]

First Peter 3:21-22 speaks of *"Jesus Christ, who has gone into heaven and is at God's right hand—with angels, authorities and powers in submission to Him."*

The following terminology is used in the Scriptures:

Thrones and Dominions (might, Greek = *dunamis*)
Principalities and Powers (powers, Greek = *exousia* [Eph. 6:12])
Archangels and Angels (angels, Gree = *aggelos*)
The three spheres include *earth, sky,* and *heaven.*
FIRST SPHERE: Seraphim/Cherubim/thrones
  (Greek = *thronos*)

SECOND SPHERES dominions (Greek = *kuriotes*)/virtues (Greek = *dunamis*)/powers (Greek = *exousia*)

THIRD SPHERE: Principalities and Powers (powers, Greek = *arche*)/archangels and angels (angels, Greek = *aggelos*)/ thrones and dominions

THE THREE HIERARCHIES OF HELL

Likewise, there is a hierarchy in hell and names to invoke hell itself. There are ranks of demons. Some say there are ten orders, others say nine. I believe the reason there is confusion about the matter is that, even during the past several years there has been a great increase of darkness and division within the hierarchy of hell. We need to remember there is deep, dark revelation that has vast and manifold meaning. It evolves. I'm so thankful that the glory of God is greater and its manifold blessings are deeper; they are a well of life.

In the end, satan will meet his doom.

> When the thousand years are over, satan will be released from his prison and will go out to deceive the nations in the four corners of the earth—Gog and Magog—to gather them for battle. In number they are like the sand on the seashore. They marched across the breadth of the earth and surrounded the camp of God's people, the city he loves. But fire came down from heaven and devoured them. And the devil, who deceived them, was thrown into the lake of burning sulfur, where the beast and the false prophet had been thrown. They will be tormented day and night for ever and ever (Revelation 20:7-10).

So when you are accused by the devil and he lies to you, you can remind him that his time is coming to an end and that he cannot have you. Amen!

Following is important and specific information regarding the three hierarchies of hell:

First Hierarchy of Hell: the Orders of Seraphim, Cherubim, and Thrones

The specialty of seraphim is revenge. Their objective is justice as they defeat their enemies. They also specialize in teaching astrology, the healing arts, and divination. As for the order of the cherubim, their specialty is fortune-telling of the past, present, and future. They have the ability to astral project and the gift of knowledge, which they use in destructive ways. The order of thrones are the rulers of black magic.

Second Hierarchy: Dominions, Principalities, and Powers

Dominions help in accessing the power of satan within an individual. They empower spiritually and psychically, and they integrate the spiritual and material worlds. Principalities influence world events. According to *dictionary.reference.com*, a principality is "a territory ruled by a prince...or from which such a title is derived; the position, authority, or jurisdiction of a prince...; sovereignty." Principalities rule over nations within a military structure. Satan is their master, and they are his generals.

According to the same reference site, *power* is "a specific capacity, faculty, or aptitude; strength or force exerted or capable of being exerted; might; the ability or official capacity to exercise control; authority; forcefulness; effectiveness."

Third Hierarchy: Virtues, Archangels, and Angels

In the natural world, we have presidents, kings, governors, mayors, etc. The dark ones also have leagues, hierarchies, levels, and degrees of darkness. Demonic kings bring forth confidence and fearlessness in their subjects and also assist in black magic. They refer to themselves by various names and titles such as prince, king, marquis, duke, earl, and president. The noble ranks of hell have five levels of demons. (There are also five levels of angels. Remember, the demonic always mimics the things of God.)

Your authority is your weapon! As you gain more understanding with regard to how satan's hierarchy operates, it will be easier to recognize the enemy. I personally feel that when we know what we're up against and we have the proper tools (through and in Christ Jesus), we are able to break down the strongholds that hold millions in their clutches. Even as we fight against pornography and gay marriage in America, I have a dream that one day we will stand strong because the belt of truth and our words will reverse the curses that have plagued humanity for centuries, brought about by satan and all his dark winged ones. Can you imagine a day when darkness will not be at the forefront of our lives? When we are no longer hindered and entrapped by satan's wiles and schemes? When families will be restored, marriages renewed, cities and towns changed by one curse being reversed? We will become armed and dangerous as we dream. Dream with me…it can happen… it is happening.

THE NINE SATANIC STATEMENTS

The next two sections are directly taken from *The Satanic Bible*, so that we can be informed, educated, and thus prepared to fight the battle and win the war.

1. satan represents indulgence, instead of abstinence!
2. satan represents vital existence, instead of spiritual pipedreams!
3. satan represents undefiled wisdom, instead of hypocritical self-deceit!

4. satan represents kindness to those who deserve it, instead of love wasted on ingrates!

5. satan represents vengeance, instead of turning the other cheek!

6. satan represents responsibility to the responsible, instead of concern for psychic vampires!

7. satan represents man as just another animal, sometimes better, more often worse than those that walk on all-fours, who, because of his "divine spiritual and intellectual development," has become the most vicious animal of all!

8. satan represents all the so-called sins, as they all lead to physical, mental, or emotional gratification!

9. satan has been the best friend the church has ever had, as he has kept it in business all these years![33]

THE NINE SATANIC SINS

According to LaVey, there are nine satanic sins.

1. *Stupidity*—The top of the list for satanic Sins. The Cardinal Sin of satanism. It's too bad that stupidity isn't painful. Ignorance is one thing, but our society thrives increasingly on stupidity. It depends on people going along with whatever they are told. The media promotes a cultivated stupidity as a posture that is not only acceptable but laudable. Satanists must learn to see through the tricks and cannot afford to be stupid.

2. *Pretentiousness*—Empty posturing can be most irritating and isn't applying the cardinal rules of Lesser Magic. On equal footing with stupidity for what keeps the money in circulation these days. Everyone's made to

feel like a big shot, whether they can come up with the goods or not.

3. *Solipsism*—Can be very dangerous for satanists. Projecting your reactions, responses and sensibilities onto someone who is probably far less attuned than you are. It is the mistake of expecting people to give you the same consideration, courtesy and respect that you naturally give them. They won't. Instead, satanists must strive to apply the dictum of "Do unto others as they do unto you." It's work for most of us and requires constant vigilance lest you slip into a comfortable illusion of everyone being like you. As has been said, certain utopias would be ideal in a nation of philosophers, but unfortunately (or perhaps fortunately, from a Machiavellian standpoint) we are far from that point.

4. *Self-deceit*—It's in the "Nine satanic Statements" but deserves to be repeated here. Another cardinal sin. We must not pay homage to any of the sacred cows presented to us, including the roles we are expected to play ourselves. The only time self-deceit should be entered into is when it's fun, and with awareness. But then, it's not self-deceit!

5. *Herd Conformity*—That's obvious from a satanic stance. It's all right to conform to a person's wishes, if it ultimately benefits you. But only fools follow along with the herd, letting an impersonal entity dictate to you. The key is to choose a master wisely instead of being enslaved by the whims of the many.

6. *Lack of Perspective*—Again, this one can lead to a lot of pain for a satanist. You must never lose sight of who and what you are, and what a threat you can be, by your very existence. We are making history right now, every day. Always keep the wider historical and social picture in mind. That is an important key to both Lesser and Greater Magic. See the patterns and fit things together as you want the pieces to fall into place. Do not be swayed by herd constraints—know that you are working on another level entirely from the rest of the world.

7. *Forgetfulness of Past Orthodoxies*—Be aware that this is one of the keys to brainwashing people into accepting something new and different, when in reality it's something that was once widely accepted but is now presented in a new package. We are expected to rave about the genius of the creator and forget the original. This makes for a disposable society.

8. *Counterproductive Pride*—That first word is important. Pride is great up to the point you begin to throw out the baby with the bathwater. The rule of satanism is: if it works for you, great. When it stops working for you, when you've painted yourself into a corner and the only way out is to say, I'm sorry, I made a mistake, I wish we could compromise somehow, then do it.

9. *Lack of Aesthetics*—This is the physical application of the Balance Factor. Aesthetics is important in Lesser Magic and should be cultivated. It is obvious that no one can collect any money off classical standards of beauty and form most of the time so they are discouraged in a consumer society, but an eye for beauty, for balance, is

an essential satanic tool and must be applied for greatest magical effectiveness. It's not what's supposed to be pleasing—it's what is. Aesthetics is a personal thing, reflective of one's own nature, but there are universally pleasing and harmonious configurations that should not be denied.[34]

The nine satanic statements as well as the nine satanic sins are a total contradiction to the Word of God, the Christian life, and the moral society that God intended for humanity. Rather than follow the precious example of our Lord Jesus Christ, who gave His life for us, and serve Him with the fruits of the Spirit in our lives, the devil and his cohorts want to lure you into believing that you will find satisfaction and fulfillment by entertaining your own flesh and serving your own selfish desires. However, the truth is, with Christ, there is love; with the devil there is only evil and hate; with Christ there is joy; with the devil there is misery and pain; with Christ you will experience peace; with the devil, only distress and worry. With Christ, you will learn patience, you will be gentle and good and kind; you will have faith, humility, and self-control. With the devil, you will know only cruelty, corruptness, distrust, suspicion, selfishness, hostility, and unpredictability. The devil wants you to condemn your soul to hell, now and forevermore.

CHAPTER 8

DELIVERANCE FROM THE DEMONS AND SPIRITS OF HELL

When the glory of God is released, angels ascend and descend from Heaven to bring the revelation that we need to do His bidding. When I'm participating in a healing service, I ask the Father to release the gift of faith, to pour it from the bowls of His throne, and to equip us with what we need. I have seen this work time and time again.

When the Lord gives us an assignment, it's our job to ask for what we need to complete the work. But if we don't step into formation, stay in cadence, and protect what He has equipped us with, we can't adequately advance His Kingdom and take dominion with all authority. I can't stress enough that we have been given weapons to use for healing and deliverance. As we learn to use these weapons, our faith increases and consequently, we use them even more effectively. Miracles, signs, and wonders are birthed out of our obedience to Him. Remember, your authority is your weapon.

For most of my Christian life, I have been active in deliverance ministry. It makes me laugh to think that my father's side of the family is Sicilian Italian mafia, and my mother's family is Blackfoot Native American. My great, great-grandfather was a chief. It's no wonder I've not shied away from battle—I have warfare in my bloodline on both sides.

EXORCISM

Throughout the years, I have been called an exorcist because I expel demons. The word *exorcism* sounds strange to me, but actually it is the truth. An exorcist performs a ceremony during which evil spirits are driven out. He or she uses prayers and religious rituals to drive away evil spirits that have possessed a person or a location. Exorcism is deliverance ministry.

> Driving out devils and demons was performed in Old Testament times: Josephus says that King Solomon's 'forms of exorcism' were used in such a situation by one Eleazar performing before the Emperor Vespasian.[35]

In recent years, parchments have been found that reveal that King Solomon was also able to expel demons. Because he was known around the world as a king with great wisdom and discernment from God, it makes sense that he had great knowledge of the spiritual world as well. However, this great king experienced a downfall, and I believe there is a warning here for all of us. Many of King Solomon's wives were pagan, non-believers of Yahweh, who led Solomon into the worship of demon gods. Thus the veil was lifted, and the presence of God was also lifted. The glory was no longer evident—in either the spirit or natural realm. Solomon became a blind seer.

King Solomon was not exempt from falling away, and neither are we. We must be conscious and very aware of the seven deadly sins—the battles we fight against:

Lucifer: pride spirit of haughtiness
Mammon: greed seducing spirit
Asmodeus: lust perverse spirit
Leviathan: envy spirit of haughtiness

Beelzebub: gluttony spirit of heaviness
Satan/Amon: wrath spirit of jealousy
Belphegor: sloth spirit of lethargy

Thousands of years ago, when Joel chapter 3 was written, believers even then were waiting for prophecy to come to pass. Today, we have more understanding of the revelatory Word of God, and we actually do see the signs and wonders about which Joel was speaking. There has been an acceleration of the anointing of the Holy Spirit, and we have witnessed some amazing moments in time—even true revival. But we must be careful. God is a God of holiness. He will not tolerate the Eli's and Jezebels. The fear of God must resonate within each of us. This is the beginning of wisdom (see Job 28:28; Ps. 111:10). Now is the time of activation.

In the New Testament, Christ also exorcised devils and demons and gave His apostles and disciples the power to do so. Saint Paul in Acts of the Apostles is reported to have driven the evil spirit out of a girl who was being used to prophesy.[36]

This girl was actually practicing divination. In today's society, she would be called a medium or psychic. Divination is the ability to know the hidden things in a person's life. It's related to the "third eye." Acts chapter 19 includes a story that gives us clear direction to not mess with the demonic realm if we are unprepared.

The early fathers of the church (Tertullian, Origen, and others) and the great Saint Thomas Aquinas, of the *Summa theologica*, and medieval Popes all speak of and defend the rite of exorcism. The Roman Catholic Church has been using exorcism ever since it cleansed in this way the catechumens who wished to become full members. The sacrament of baptism is a rite of exorcism. So is the blessing of the water used in baptism, sanctifying of churches and holy water and holy oil and altars and holy vessels, and so on.

This reminds us that devils and demons have long been thought to reside in objects as well as in persons, somewhat the way gods lived in trees…[or haunted houses].

The Roman Catholic Church undertakes to exorcise even non-communicants and ex-communicants. In an emergency, any Catholic can perform an exorcism, though increasingly the church has restricted exorcism and calls upon ordinaries (superiors) to select only careful and well-adjusted priests for the rite.

All priests are exorcists. Exorcist is the third of the four minor orders leading up to Holy Orders, the ordination of a priest. In the Roman Catholic Church, there are ranks of church ministry. Exorcist is one of the minor ranks thought to be lower than the major orders, or Holy Orders.

Exorcism is simply a prayer to God to banish the creatures…[that] torment mankind.[37]

Every deliverance is different. Devils and demons do not go quietly, and the rite of exorcism is very dangerous if you don't know what you're doing. You can cause many problems for the person or for yourself. This is the reason that Matthew 12:44-45 states that if you don't close all the doors, even more darkness can enter into a person's house. The "doors" here are various demonic entities. "House" refers to one's body.

Exorcism is performed with…the laying on of hands (a traditional method of conveying power or blessing), the sign of the cross, the Holy Name, the cursing of The Devil (with demands to unclean spirits to depart), and the reading of Holy Writ.[38]

We must go after whatever spiritual aspect we're dealing with, depending on the circumstances—that is, divination, an unclean spirit, a perverse spirit, a spirit of fear, or any other number of spirits. We need to go after the seed, curse the tree to the root, command it to go, dry up, and die. Then we are able to replace the dark fruit with the manifestations of God's love. Galatians chapter 5 lists the fruits of the Holy Spirit—love, joy, peace, patience, gentleness, goodness, faith, meekness (humility), and temperance (self-control)—which is needed to fill that once dark place with the light of Christ. We can close those open doors and fill the house with the presence and anointing of God.

> There used to be a *"Book of Exorcisms"*. Now the formula for exorcism is in the *"Rituale Romanum"* approved by 17th century authorities and reprinted often, though not usually consulted by the laity. [It] is 'the book' used in exorcism by 'bell, book and candle.' (see also: "The Roman Catholic Exorcism" [Translated from the *"Rituale Romanum"*, first published in the reign of Paul V])[39]

DEMONS

Let's look at what the encyclopedia has to say about a demon:

> [A demon is a] supernatural being, spirit, or force capable of influencing human lives, usually by evil means. Demons have played a role in the traditions of most religions and also have appeared in mythology and literature. Exorcism, the practice of expelling demons that possess people or places, has been carried out by many religions, usually by a person with special authority. The study of demons is called demonology.

The belief in evil spirits and their ability to influence the lives of people dates from [the Garden of Eden]. Many early people believed that spirits occupied all elements of nature. Evil spirits or demons were the spirits of ancestors who brought harm to living people. Societies that practiced ancestor worship sought to influence the actions of both good and bad spirits. Some ancient societies, including those in Egypt and Babylonia (now Iraq), believed that such spirits were responsible for the functions of the body and that demons caused specific illnesses.

Spirits and demonic beings became an important part of Hinduism, the religion of India. Hindu scriptures called the *Vedas*, composed between about 1500 BC and about 1000 BC, describe a variety of evil beings, including the *asuras* and the *panis*, who harm people and work against the Hindu gods. The word *demon* originated from an ancient Greek term, *daimon*, which referred to beings whose special powers placed them between people and the gods. These beings had the ability either to improve people's lives or carry out the punishment of the gods.

Basic Christian ideas about demons originated from references to evil beings or "unclean spirits" in the Old Testament of the Bible. By the Middle Ages, Christian theology had developed an elaborate hierarchy of angels, who were associated with God, and fallen angels, or demons, who were led by satan. Satan himself was considered the original fallen angel. In most English versions of the Bible, the term demon is translated as devil, and in the New Testament, demon is identified with an evil spirit.

Islam also developed a complex system of demons. Muslim writings describe a group of evil beings, called *jinn*, who cause destruction and preside over places where evil activities take place. The original jinn was called Iblis, who was cast out by Allah for refusing to worship Adam, the first man.

Demons also have become part of folklore throughout the world. Many of these demons have peculiar qualities. They include such familiar creatures as vampires, who suck the blood of living victims. Another variety of demon, the Japanese *oni*, are said to bring on storms. In Scotland legendary *kelpies* haunt pools, waiting to drown unwary travelers.[40]

These demonic beings are not merely the stuff of fairy tales or folklore. When stories are passed down from generation to generation they become either exaggerated or watered down. Since the Salem witch trials ended in the 1700's, a common belief in demons or evil spirits has declined. Unfortunately, this mistake has been made among the Christian community.

SEVEN PRINCIPALITIES OF DEMONS

Witches are taught that there are seven high-ranking Principalities of hell. Why are they being taught this information? To curse and destroy our works. And yet many claim they are "good witches." The reason I am exposing this information is to give Christians a greater understanding of how the different levels of satanism work. Satan has witches and a hierarchy. For example, there are five brides of satan. Each bride is assigned a different element of the earth. If we see our children falling into dark areas, then as parents and responsible Christians, we can step up and step in to help those who don't know how to fight.

Following are terms that are very important to know when combatting evil:

1. *Rege*: the General of the occult, Rege deals with drugs such as marijuana, hashish, cocaine, speed, LSD, peyote, and mescaline. These are the drugs of sorcery. They attack the mind and open it up to demonic access. Rege is also responsible for seeing to it that music is hexed and cursed.

2. *Larz*: the demon of sexual lust, homosexuality, bisexuality, adultery, and any fantasy concerning sexual pleasures. Because of Larz, pornography (including "hardcore") is everywhere—the internet, movies, magazines, and books.

3. *Bacchus*: the demon of addictions, including drugs, alcohol, or anything else that keeps a person bound.

4. *Pan*: the demon of the mind. Because of Pan, mental illness is on the rise, including depression and suicide. Have you noticed that it can be spiritually deadly when a person becomes depressed or feels rejected?

5. *Medit*: the demon of hate, murder, killing, war, jealousy, envy, and gossip. This demon is active in society today. Just turn on the news, read the paper, or buy a tabloid, and you will see Medit at work.

6. *Set*: the demon of death. He influences everything from war and terrorism to murder and rage throughout the world. The twentieth century was the most violent and bloody in world history.

7. *The "Christian" Demon*: also referred to as the no-name demon. He is so powerful that most witches won't even call upon him. As long as we Christians continue to talk about one another through gossiping and slander, there will be strife within the church and among the brethren. So, in actuality, we make it easy for demons to sit back and enjoy watching us do the work for the spirits of darkness. The no-name demon will try to weaken a Christian's walk with the Lord by encouraging him to

become "average," lukewarm, content, non-committed, so that he fails to live up to church commitments such as tithing, soul-winning, church participation, fear of God, and much more. Could the persistent activities of this demon be responsible for mayhem within the church? Yes!

CASTING SPELLS

Since the times of the ancients, there have been those who draw power off the earth's elements. In the Book of Genesis, God Himself breathed into the ground and made man. The moon influences the earth's atmosphere, causing the seas and rivers to shift. Those who practice magick, likewise, use power from the elements.

Witches do cast spells and their magic is carried out inside a circle. In addition, they often recite specific chants.[41] Witches do incantations in order to invoke dark, evil spirits. One of the best references I can give you is the story of King Saul.

> Then said Saul unto his servants, Seek me a woman that hath a familiar spirit, that I may go to her, and enquire of her. And his servants said to him, Behold, there is a woman that hath a familiar spirit at Endor (1 Samuel 28:7 KJV).

> Witches also walk or dance around the circle and always signify the elements during their rituals. Examples include lighting incense for air, lighting candles for fire, pouring water for water, and pouring dirt or using their crystals for earth. Many witches end the casting with a ritual at the altar. Often this involves invoking the spirit of life as represented by salt (such as pouring salt). And usually this ends with a dedication or prayer to their deity (or deities). If the circle is used for casting magick, the witch will dedicate it to their god/goddess.[42]

Witches use not just incense and candles but many different elements to mix an elixir or cast a spell. The information presented here is real. It is identical to firsthand accounts by ex-witches who want others to understand demonic evil and its power. You never want to find yourself in these types of occult activities. It's a serious and often deadly matter to play with the dark side.

A FAMILY'S NIGHTMARE

At first, a Ouija board might seem like an innocent game. Yet it will open a door that will release a dark force beyond your imagination. Like a poltergeist, it will pull a person into another dimension that no one is ready for. It can and will cause a lot of problems for the participants, who seek information as they question the board for answers. There is a demon attached to the game that speaks through the board as it spells out words, giving the players the answers they seek.

Years ago, I went to the home of a family to do a spiritual house-cleaning/blessing. The visit turned into a deliverance session for the entire family, and all generational curses were broken. There was an innocence about the high school girls who had played this game—a simple board game that opened many doors into the unknown. Fear gripped the entire family once they realized what they had done by invoking evil spirits. They were so afraid that they decided to throw the game into the fireplace and let it burn—but it wouldn't burn. That night, they threw it in the garbage can, but the next morning it was back on the porch, though no one had touched it.

The youngest daughter, Karen, who was 14, was being sexually violated by a perverse spirit throughout the two-week ordeal. She would be violently pulled out of bed or the bed would shake as though the earth were quaking. When this began happening, the family was frightened; but when objects started levitating, suspended in midair, they knew they could not handle the situation. Even praying and reading the Bible wasn't enough. The final straw took place in the kitchen; dishes began flying. Glasses broke as they were hurled against the walls. I was called in to assess and was asked to help this family. Through the experience, I learned much that was (and still is) very valuable.

After days of assessing the situation, I brought in a few of my colleagues. With the power that comes only through fasting and prayer, we were able to close the doors. But a week later, I was called back in. A certain living room window was wet, dripping with water. We went outside to look at the rain gutters to see if perhaps there was a spout near the window, but that wasn't the problem. Karen had reopened the door, not through the Ouija board, but through another dark power—seducing and perverse spirits. We had a battle on our hands.

> When an evil spirit comes out of a man, it goes through arid places seeking rest and does not find it. Then it says, "I will return to the house I left." When it arrives, it finds the house unoccupied, swept clean and put in order. Then it goes and takes with it seven other spirits more wicked than itself, and they go in and live there. And the final condition of that man is worse than the first. That is how it will be with this wicked generation (Matthew 12:43-45).

The twelve manifestations of the unclean spirit are very clear. Just as angels are on assignment, so are demons. The networking that goes on in the spiritual world is parallel to that of the natural one in which we live. Once we were able to defeat the stronghold—the seducing spirit, life really turned around for this family. The curse with which the mother had been plagued during her whole life was finally broken. The familiar spirit had no rightful entry point into her life or the lives of her children—except for Karen. The fatal attraction of the perverse spirit was so strong that she ran away from home. The last time the family heard from her, she was into witchcraft, drugs, stripping, and prostitution. As crazy as this might sound, you need to understand that she was in love with this demon. In her mind, no one and nothing would ever change that. Karen reopened the door, and that was her choice. Sad but true, sometimes people who have opened the doors do not want them closed. They love the power of the magick and the intrigue of the dark side.

When the unclean spirit is gone out of a man, he walketh through dry places, seeking rest, and findeth none. Then he saith, I will return into my house from whence I came out; and when he is come, he findeth it empty, swept, and garnished. Then goeth he, and taketh with himself seven other spirits more wicked than himself, and they enter in and dwell there: and the last state of that man is worse than the first. Even so shall it be also unto this wicked generation (Matthew 12:43-45).

MANIFESTATIONS OF EVIL SPIRITS

Let's first review the following types of evil spirits and their definitions and descriptions.

Diviner: Witch or warlock; soothsayer; observer of times (almanacs and horoscopes).

Enchanter: Magician; witch or wizard; one who practices witchcraft and sorcery.

Hypnotist: Charmer; medium; one who consults with familiar spirits.

Necromancer: One who consults with the dead.

Conjurer: One who summons or commands demons to appear.

Astrologer/Stargazer: One who predicts the future according to the position of the planets, sun, and moon.

Divinatory has to do with the method or practice of attempting to foretell the future or discovering the unknown through omens, oracles, or supernatural powers to seek knowledge.

Divination is the result of a familiar spirit. This entity operates through our past, and continually brings the past to our attention, so that we are always defiled, depressed, and/or under a weight of guilt and remorse. We are bound and chained. We're held captive and not able to see the future. Additionally, peer pressure—and wanting to be accepted by others—is a powerful force. Many people give in to it because it seems easier to walk in darkness and even in defilement rather than to face rejection. Many young people are gripped by the pressures of society to the point that the defilement affects all areas of their life—family, school, church, and community.

> Necromancy…is a form of divination in which the practitioner seeks to summon "operative spirits" or "spirits of divination," for multiple reasons, from spiritual protection to wisdom. The word *necromancy* derives from the Greek "dead" and… "divination."
>
> However, since the Renaissance, necromancy has come to be associated more broadly with black magic and demon-summoning in general, sometimes losing its earlier, more specialized meaning. By popular etymology, *nekromantia* became *nigromancy* "black arts," and Johannes Hartlieb (1456) lists demonology in general under the heading. Eliphas Levi, in his book *"Dogma et Ritual"*, states that necromancy is the evoking of aerial bodies (aeromancy).[43]

Let's look at the grimoire once more:

> A grimoire is a textbook of magic. Books of this genre, typically giving instructions for invoking angels

or demons, performing divination and gaining magical powers, have circulated throughout Europe since the Middle Ages.

Magicians were frequently persecuted by the Church, so their journals were kept hidden to prevent them from being burned. Such books contain astrological correspondences, lists of angels and demons, directions on casting charms and spells, mixing medicines, summoning unearthly entities, and making talismans. Magical books in almost any context, especially books of magical spells, are also called grimoires.[44]

Now let's consider the following information regarding magicians:

A magician is a person skilled in the mysterious and hidden art of magic, the ability to attain objectives, acquire knowledge, or perform works of wonder using supernatural or non-rational means.

Some modern magicians, such as Aleister Crowley and those who follow the traditions of the Hermetic Order of the Golden Dawn and Ordo Templi Orientis, describe magic in rational terms, using definitions, postulates and theorems.

The latter kind of magician can also be referred to as an enchanter, sorcerer, wizard, mage, magus, necromancer, or thaumaturgist. These overlapping terms may be distinguished by some traditions or some fiction writers. When such distinctions are made, sorcerers are more often practitioners of evocations or black magic, and there may be variations on level and type of power associated with each name.[45]

There are covens in every city, and I'm sure in many junior high and high schools all over this great nation and around the world. It's easy for the younger generation to be pulled in by seducing spirits.

THE LEVELS OF HELL

There are many, many descriptions of hell. Indeed, God has much to say about it as well.

> Hell, according to many religious beliefs, is a place of suffering during afterlife where the wicked or un-righteous souls are punished. Hell is usually depicted as underground. Within Islam and Christianity, Hell is traditionally depicted as fiery and painful, inflicting guilt and suffering. Some other traditions, however, portray Hell as cold and gloomy. Existence after life is not concrete in Judaism and may be portrayed as a state of neutrality, an eternal nothingness ("sheol", often mis-translated as hell), simply non-life....
>
> Religions with a linear divine history often depict Hell as endless.... Punishment in Hell typically corre-sponds to sins committed in life. Sometimes these dis-tinctions are specific...and sometimes they are general, with sinners being relegated to one or more chamber of Hell or level of suffering....[46]
>
> In Christianity, faith and repentance determine our eternal destiny. Despite some common depictions of Hell, it is a fiery inferno. The damned are eternally separated from God. Some believe hell includes nine circles (or levels) and that the ninth (innermost) circle is actually "a frozen lake of blood and guilt."

Hell is often portrayed as populated with demons who torment the damned.... In contrast to Hell, other general types of afterlives are abodes of the dead and paradises. Abodes of the dead are neutral places for all the dead...rather than prisons of punishment for sinners.... Modern understandings of Hell often depict it abstractly, as a state of loss rather than as fiery torture literally under the ground.[47]

What does God's Holy Bible have to say about hell?

They will throw them into the fiery furnace, where there will be weeping and gnashing of teeth.... Then He will say to those on His left, "Depart from Me, you who are cursed, into the eternal fire prepared for the devil and his angels" (Matthew 13:42; 25:41).

And I saw an angel coming down out of heaven, having the key to the Abyss and holding in his hand a great chain. He seized the dragon, that ancient serpent, who is the devil, or satan, and bound him for a thousand years. He threw him into the Abyss, and locked and sealed it over him, to keep him from deceiving the nations anymore until the thousand years were ended. After that, he must be set free for a short time (Revelation 20:1-3).

Twice I have had visions of hell. It was very real and very overwhelming. One time, I saw many people falling into an abyss of darkness. They spiraled downward very quickly, yet I saw it happen in slow motion. I was led to observe one man who was full of darkness. He was thrown into a chamber—a small room where many were being tortured. In this crevice of hell, people were chained to their sin. I was able to see the perversions of people's minds; they could never be satisfied. The lust of their sin was perpetual. They were screaming for the lust of their flesh to be satisfied. They were enslaved to the darkness. They could not be and will never be satisfied.

As the vision continued, I saw people swimming in a lake of fire. They could not get out and were unable to get to land. Somehow, their features were recognizable though they were invisible. I couldn't see skin or hair—only a tracing of their physical bodies. I could see the torment on their faces, and I knew it was an endless torture. I believe that they had known God was real but had rejected Him. They had heard the truth and yet had denied Christ. They had fulfilled the passions and lusts of their flesh on earth only to face the greatest torture of all.

> *The fool says in his heart, "There is no God." They are corrupt, their deeds are vile; there is no one who does good. The LORD looks down from heaven on the sons of men to see if there are any who understand, any who seek God. All have turned aside, they have together become corrupt; there is no one who does good, not even one* (Psalm 14:1-3).

The people I saw in the vision had known that Jesus was the Messiah, the Son of the living God. He had offered them life and had wanted them to receive His love, but now it was too late. I have thought, *Lord, how Your heart must break for those was are lost, who are in darkness.* Every day we must make the choice as to whether or not we will pick up our cross and follow Him.

As the world descends into greater darkness, sin will attempt to draw us into fulfilling the lusts of the mind and flesh. The enemy twists and perverts; this is why so many are not being set free. That's where our responsibilities come in. With knowledge as God gives it, we can do *all things.* But keep in mind that Jeremiah 12:5 states, *"If you have raced with men on foot and they have worn you out, how can you compete with horses? If you stumble in safe country, how will you manage in the thickets by the Jordan?"* In other words, if we can't keep up with foot soldiers, how will we be able to make it in the time of horses and chariots (which indicates high warfare)?

And from the days of John the Baptist until now the kingdom of heaven suffereth violence, and the violent take it by force (Matthew 11:12 KJV).

We will set the captives free!

Then death and Hades were thrown into the lake of fire. The lake of fire is the second death. If anyone's name was not found written in the book of life, he was thrown into the lake of fire (Revelation 20:14-15).

The Bible provides many warnings and portrays a terrible picture of the final destiny of the lost. It describes unspeakable trouble and distress.

There will be trouble and distress for every human being who does evil: first for he Jew, then for the Gentile (Romans 2:9).

"Then the king told the attendants, "Tie him hand and foot, and throw him outside, into the darkness, where there will be weeping and gnashing of teeth" (Matthew 22:13).

They will be punished with everlasting destruction and shut out from the presence of the Lord and from the majesty of His power (2 Thessalonians 1:9).

This is how it will be at the end of the age. The angels will come and separate the wicked from the righteous and throw them into the fiery furnace, where there will be weeping and gnashing of teeth (Matthew 13:49-50).

If your hand causes you to sin, cut it off. It is better for you to enter life maimed than with two hands to go into hell, where the fire never goes out [some manuscripts say, "where their worm does not die, and the fire is not quenched."] (Mark 9:43).

And the smoke of their torment rises for ever and ever.

There is no rest day or night... (Revelation 14:11).
    It is a dreadful thing to fall into the hands of the living God (Hebrews 10:31).

The early New Testament Church possessed a sincere love for those living in sin. Many who walked and worked with Jesus saw the truth and passed it on after His ascension. Likewise, we also must keep loving people who choose to live in sin. But we can't rescue those in great darkness if we don't know exactly what we're doing. We must have help from those who are equipped. Many times, one who is weak and unprepared but who tries to help a friend who is really "going through it" will be drawn away from the Father. Those who aren't adequately prepared and who haven't first built a deep foundation through knowledge and training have the potential to fall into the sins of those they want to help.

We must put the Gospel into action. John 3:16 states that *"God so loved the world that He gave His only begotten Son, that whoever believes in Him should not perish [die] but have everlasting life"* (NKJV). We must reclaim our first love with holy fire and passion for truth and justice. Righteousness must be our number-one priority. Our goal must be to restore holiness and the fear of God to the priests and pulpits of His temple.

CHAPTER 9

LOVE THEM BACK TO LIFE

Here is Lani's story, told in her own words:

I was born into this world seeing spirits. Even at a young age, this gift was so sharp and so real—the visions were so clear that I sometimes didn't know the difference between the physical and spiritual. I heard voices, saw shadows, and had nightmares so vivid that even before I was old enough to talk I woke up screaming. The visions and nightmares only got worse as time passed.

I had one friend through it all—the only one who believed and protected me—and that was my "guardian angel"—Seth. He was my constant friend and comforter, talking me through every aspect of my life. He taught me how to protect myself from the dark beings that swirled around me and tortured me day and night. He also taught me how to change my dreams and gain power over them, as well as to "dream-walk" into other people's dreams and alter them.

I grew up in a sad, chaotic household with a monster for a father and an overwhelmed mother who tried to keep us all together and love us while appeasing the illogical and crazy requests of my father. We went to church every Sunday, every holiday, and every feast day...we were very involved. I saw God there, and I knew Jesus, but I also learned that most of the Christians I knew had absolutely no discernment at all.

They told me how lucky I was to have such a nice father who loved the Lord so much. They said he was one of the finest people they knew. They said this as I stood there covered in scars inflicted by this "nice" father who was "so close to the Lord" and wondered what exactly they were talking about.

I gradually learned to rely more on Seth and less on the people around me, primarily because he made everything tolerable. The only other person on whom I relied was Jesus. I had an incredible relationship with Jesus as a child. Night after night, I spoke to Him non-stop, and He came to me in spirit—bright and loving; He even sat on my bed. It was just Jesus and me as I rambled on and on about school and life and my family. But as time passed, Seth made himself more visible and approachable, and eventually I couldn't tell the difference between him and Jesus.

After my father finally left us, we never had to see him—except at church. This didn't help my growing dissatisfaction with religion. The services seemed cold and more about lip service and ritual than anything else. The Holy Spirit was spoken about and respected but not present. He was someone who *would* come if need be rather than someone who was always there.

By the time I reached my teenage years, I had abandoned the Church completely in favor of the more spiritual path that Seth was willing to reveal to me. For hours at a time, I would hear his voice in my head as he told me more information than most people could learn in a lifetime. He offered me what the Church hadn't: power and control. The Church had showed me a faraway, benevolent being who heard our prayers. It had shown me a God who died for sins we continued to commit and a Holy Ghost who haunted the earth, spooking the evil into goodness.

But, strangely enough, I never heard about the power of Jesus. At church, we never read anything in the Bible that promoted the idea that He was still actively involved and would present Himself to us in full power and glory if only we asked Him to. I never learned that the relationship I had with Seth—who had become a loving, powerful ally and comforter, a best friend, father, teacher, and guardian—was actually the sort of relationship we were supposed to have with Jesus. Seth had taken Jesus' place in my life and my heart and was doing a fine job as a counterfeit Christ. I had no idea that he was a familiar spirit. I had no idea that such a thing even existed. Those around me passed him off as a mental disorder or imaginary friend.

Seth led me to other like-minded individuals, those who were spiritually aware and didn't think of me as a freak. They all could do what I could do: read minds, alter environments, and speak with and see spirits. They were witches and goddesses. They made sense to me. I decided I could understand this life, and even though the idea of goddesses seemed odd to me, I had had quite enough of males.

It was difficult for me to simply forget about Jesus, and I couldn't proclaim Him a myth as did the pagans I dealt with. Instead, I convinced myself that God, Jehovah, and all that went with Him was just one option out of many possibilities and that I would just quietly slip out of one pantheon into the other.

The Morrighan, a Celtic war goddess, became my new god. She came to me with a euphoric power that made me want to breathe her and be her, and she wanted the same of me. Unbeknownst to me as I lived out the fantastic lie that I was in control, I was being trained to be the Morrighan. I would be her avatar; I would become possessed by her forever so she could access this world.

During the next ten or twelve years, I worked my way up, learning everything I could from anyone who would teach me. The power within me grew as more spirits flocked to me, wanting to be my slaves. Drunk with the feeling of control and pride, I allowed them in. Soon I could tell them ahead of time what I wanted done (and to whom) and be confident that, when I walked into a room, it had already been accomplished—even before I could finish my thoughts. Seth, my constant companion, naturally ruled over the other spirits and kept them in line for me. Jealous and protective, he made sure no one entered my world of whom he didn't approve.

I became a high priestess, yet still I was not satisfied. I wanted to consume the world, and Seth was willing to take me to that level. I did good things, or so I thought. I read Tarot cards for a living in an attempt to steer people in the right direction. I carried out spells for people in trouble, teaching them, empowering them, and converting them to Wicca. Who wouldn't want to have what I had? It seemed I was finally in complete control of my life. But nothing lasts forever, including lies—even complicated, demonically powered ones.

Eventually I made a mistake, and it was almost deadly. I helped a Christian. I had a very good friend at work; we were friends despite our religious differences. We simply didn't talk about the issue. One night, a demon attacked her in her dreams. Seth had taught me to enter people's dreams, but sometimes it happened by accident. That night, I fell into my friend's dream and saw the demon. It was choking her to death. I interfered, calling it out and making it leave, and then I woke up. The next day at work, my friend and I discussed the mutual dream. I had saved her life (physically as well as spiritually) as far as she was concerned. Shortly thereafter, everything began to unravel rather quickly.

For many years, I had not encountered anything in the physical or spiritual realm that was bigger and stronger than I was. I had begun to believe that perhaps there wasn't anything more powerful, but as I departed from this friend that day at work, I realized that what I had banished in that dream was not merely an evil spirit, but a full-blown demon…and now this demon was back and ready to pay me a visit. I felt a finger tap me on my forehead, slide down the left side of my face, and then tap me on the temple. Five seconds later, at the age of 26, I had a stroke.

I tried to call for help, but nothing but nonsense came out of my mouth as the entire left side of my body went numb. I was rushed to the hospital. The doctors kept me for hours and hours, trying to find physical evidence of a stroke, but the usual scar tissue in the brain did not appear in the scans. I knew they were wasting their time. I knew what had happened, and I walked out of that hospital thoroughly outraged. Whatever had just tried to kill me became my only focus. The enemy of one's enemy is a friend, so I went looking for Jesus.

Things began to change after that. I wasn't looking for a relationship with Jesus, just the power to destroy the demon. Of course, it didn't work that way.

Seth was very quiet during all of this. When I finally found some Christians I could trust—earnest followers and seekers of Jesus—he sort of took a vacation. Since I had believed the lie in my mind that he was my "guardian angel" as a child, I simply shoved him back into that role. But my new Christian friends knew all about the spirit realm and familiar spirits, and they had the Holy Spirit. I saw real power for the first time, and I wanted it. Seth saw this as a betrayal, and so decided that it was time for me to die.

One day while in the home of some friends, one particular friend, Sean, bravely broached the subject of Seth. As soon as I thought of Seth, it seemed that his spell was broken. He panicked and began to choke me from the inside out—with my own hands. On their feet, ever loyal and ever trustworthy, my friends led me out of the darkness, stopped Seth in his tracks, and delivered me. Sean ignored the danger that Seth, a very ancient demon, presented; with amazing bravery, he helped me find Jesus, and I was born again. Sean's sister, Braann, used her extraordinary gift of healing to keep me alive during the deliverance and to seal me with the Holy Spirit when it was over.

I will never forget it. When this thing that had controlled me my whole life with lies and deceit turned on me and attempted to end my life, the Lord—whom I had denied, blasphemed, and ignored, and whom I absolutely did not deserve—personally showed up to take Seth down. Once I was safe in His arms, I realized that Jesus had been waiting my whole life for this.

He had enjoyed driving Seth out of me and into eternal chains. He came for me even though He didn't have to. That was the moment I understood true love, and I probably will never stop tearing up when I feel His presence—and I wouldn't want to.

It helps me to remember that there isn't any place or any distance I can be taken that Jesus cannot find me and bring me home. I am the 100th sheep, the lost coin. The angels sang the day I got saved and brought my whole self, well-trained in the enemy's camp, to the Father to serve Him until my death. I have seen and known beings and things that other people can't even conceive of, and I promise you that there is nothing bigger or more powerful or more beautiful than Jesus. When I discovered this, I didn't long for control anymore, so I gave it to Him, and I will never regret it.

I Pledge My Allegiance... The only difference between what I did as a witch and what I do as a follower of Jesus concerns whom I give my allegiance to. When I defected from the enemy camp to the Body of Christ, I waited for miraculous changes. I also expected all my powers, talents, and abilities in the spirit realm to disappear and leave me a nice, normal, church-going woman.

Yeah, right. I ignored those powers, talents, and abilities in the spirit realm in order to fit in and pass muster among some of the Christians who fostered me after my deliverance. I did pretty well for a long time by shoving myself into the neat little box they offered me and expected me to stay in. But honestly, this amounted to just switching shackles. Why, exactly, did I do this? In all my times of prayer and meditation, the Father never, ever mentioned that I should change, forget everything, or stop anything. It was the well-meaning churchgoers around me who suggested I not be so loud. They implied that I must start out as a baby Christian and slowly work my way up in rank.

I had been a general in the army of darkness—an avatar for a goddess. I had been power incarnate—yet I was supposed to start over, and I was deemed unqualified to speak about the spirit realm. I had been the mistress of a demon and a tamer of spirits and had successfully navigated my way around the spirit realm as if I owned the place—yet I was expected to keep my mouth shut about what I knew because not everyone was "ready" to hear what I had to say.

People better get ready. The enemy is ready...why aren't we?

WE MUST PICK UP OUR WEAPONS

The pagans are passing out our inheritance like candy to whoever looks their way while we are throwing our weapons down because they resemble what these thieves have and use as if they were their own. Essentially, too many Christians have been bringing fists to a gunfight. And when they arrive at the gunfight, they see the enemy well-armed and decide that it's too much to handle. They sense that there is a loaded and ready weapon pointing at their heads, so they cover their faces with their hands, instruct everyone else to take care of the problem, and then pretend the problem doesn't even exist. They want to believe that, if they squeeze their eyes shut really tight and say the sinner's prayer, they'll be exempt from the fight. And later, as they fall down, one by one, like trash tossed to the curb, other Christians wonder what these fallen ones did to "deserve" it, even as they put their own hands over their faces and wait for their own demise. So how about if we all take our hands away from our faces, look down at our feet, and discover what we have discarded?

WE MUST LEARN ABOUT WICCA AND WITCHCRAFT

Wicca is a neopagan, nature-based religion, with distinctive ritual forms, seasonal observances and religious, magical, and ethical precepts. Wiccans practice a form of witchcraft, but not all witches are Wiccan.[48]

Wiccans worship both a god and goddess. Their theory is that everything on the earth has both a male and female counterpart, so why shouldn't the creator? The basic idea of Wicca is to harness universal energy in order to improve one's life and circumstances while offering this service to both pagans and non-pagans who seek their help. There is only one law of ethics that they follow—the "Wiccan Rede," which states, "Do as ye will, as long as ye harm none." I can't say this is such a bad statement, and it's probably more well-meaning that most other religious tenets; however, as long as someone is doing what he or she wills, with no regard or respect for our Father in Heaven, it doesn't really matter how good his or her acts seem to be. Anything done without His permission and out of His timing is sin. Wiccans also believe in the threefold law of return: if you break the Wiccan Rede, whatever harm you do will return to you three times over. This idea is much like that of Karma.

The major misconception about Wiccans and other pagans is that they worship satan. Inadvertently they do; anyone who is not with Christ is against Him, but Wiccans do not want to have anything to do with either God or the devil. They have taken themselves out of the equation altogether. Witches worship a god and a goddess, and most are more concerned with the goddess, which is why Wicca is particularly appealing to women as well as those who have a problem with father figures or male authority in general. In the Wiccan pantheon, the god is reduced to the paramour and consort of the goddess, who rules the universe, seasons, and all supernatural abilities. He also changes with the seasons. Though he is not in any way powerless, he is beholden to the goddess's desires. Hence, you will find many pagans who worship both the god and goddess, or just the goddess, but rarely will you find a witch who worships the god alone.

The danger is that most Christians believe that the Wiccan god and goddess are not real and that they therefore cannot do any harm. They falsely believe that magic spells, which are spoken to these "false idols," are mere acts of lip service to the empty air and that they have no real effect. But I assure you that these deities are absolutely real and that they can most certainly harm anyone, Christian or not.

These are ancient, ancient demons who have forgotten they were ever angels. Over time, they have taken on the personas and names given to them by their worshippers until they have become the embodiment of the gods and goddesses of the Greek, Roman, Celtic, and Egyptian cultures, as well as others. So look up any name you remember from mythology class, and you can be sure that, if you were to call up that entity, a real demon would answer you. Instead of possessing people, they have possessed these cultural archetypes and act accordingly. And just as the gods of mythology interact with each other in the ancient stories, so they play the same parts in reality. For example, if a witch chooses the Egyptian Isis as his or her patron goddess, Isis expects the witch to choose her husband, Osiris, as his or her patron god.

Biblical verses show that the Ephesians' devotion to Diana was so great that the Christians in Rome considered her their greatest rival. The multi-breasted statue of Diana at the temple displayed her capability to nourish all creatures and provide for them. She was known by many names including Queen of Heaven; the Great Goddess; Lunar Virgin; Mother of Animals; Lady of Wild Creatures; the Huntress; Patroness of Childbirth, Nursing and Healing. Worship to this great goddess was the impetus for one of the largest and grandest temples built at Ephesus in Turkey—one of the Seven Wonders of the Ancient World. Followers, admirers, and detractors have written about her, from the stories of Troy to the Bible, in which she is referred to as the "great goddess." As the story goes, she taught magick and witches were born.It is imperative that, as Christians, we do not throw around or casually use these ancient names, because they have real and powerful demons attached to them. They also have human followers who possess a much better grasp of spiritual warfare than does the Church. The enemy attacks us day and night because we have given our allegiance to the Lord. On one hand, the Wiccan deities are less concerned with Christians than they are with gaining worshippers, though they draw them away from God in the process. On the other hand, they are narcissistic and driven by selfishness, and so when one of their followers, a witch, is in any way disturbed, they will lash out at the culprit until the witch is satisfied—not just until they themselves are satisfied, but until the full extent of human anger and rage are sated. Consequently, Christians plagued by witchcraft usually have no idea from where it is coming or how to fight it; half the time, they don't even realize that there is even a battle in progress.

Wicca is not always hidden and practiced behind closed doors. You must realize it is viewed as a valid, modern religion and is accepted by the U.S. government as such. Wicca consists of more than covens in the woods; it includes worldwide churches and organizations. Wicca is just as—if not more—organized and popular than many other major world religions. There is no such thing as a lone witch. In fact, there are denominations of Wicca. Just as the Church has been splintered by doctrine, so has Wicca, the difference being that the various factions of Wicca are willing to work with each other amiably, while most Christian groups are not. This unity makes them strong, as they have at their disposal not just their own gods but also the gods of other covens. There is no end to their reinforcements. They also often work with others who practice witchcraft, folk magic, and sorcery.

CEREMONY AND RITUAL

Wiccans follow a seasonal cycle of rituals called "The Wheel of the Year." There are eight major ceremonies (or "sabbats") in the year, including four fire rituals called "greater sabbats" and four minor "esbats." The dates of these rituals coincide with many familiar holidays that we celebrate as well as folklore-driven days that we don't realize are related to witchcraft. Although Easter and Christmas are obviously unique to Christianity, the dates on which we celebrate them were originally chosen to coincide with pagan high days for ease of conversion during the Middle Ages. In the same way, some of the Catholic saints were originally pagan gods; for example, the British St. Brigid (or St. Brigit) was actually a Celtic goddess.

Significant Dates

February 2	Imbolc	Groundhog day
March 19-22	Ostara	Easter
May 1	Beltane	May Day
June 19-23	Midsummer	Saint Alban's day
August 1	Lughnasadh	Procession of the Cross Feast
September 21-24	Mabon	Matthew the Evangelist Day
October 31	Samhain	Halloween
December 20-23	Yule	Christmas

There are two more ceremonies worth mentioning: handfasting and wiccaning. Handfasting is essentially marriage; however, "until death do us part" is replaced with "as long as love lasts." Wiccaning is the equivalent of infant baptism. When a child is born, he or she is dedicated to the mother goddess, and the parents swear to raise the child in the Wiccan way until a certain age at which he or she either chooses another path or continues on the pagan one.

A COMPARISON OF SPIRITUAL GIFTS

The similarities between the rituals of a church service and a pagan sabbat are so confused and interwoven that it is impossible to determine which came first, and honestly it no longer matters. The issue is often just another excuse to debate doctrine and divide ourselves by asking, for example, "Which came first—the Christmas or the Yule?"

One Wiccan law concerning the spiritual realm is "As above, so below," which explains their use of spell components and tools. For instance, candlelight represents the eternal light of life. Symbolic magical items such as corn dollies and amulets physically represent the instructions to be carried out in the spirit realm by familiar spirits who have been sent out. This counterfeits the words of Jesus, who said, *"Whatever you loose on earth will be loosed in heaven"* (Matt. 16:19b; 18:18b). Are you beginning to see the similarities? Notice that the demonic realm always twists and perverts Scripture to deceive and lure with counter-religion.

Traditional Wiccan ceremonies take place in a temple in which the door faces east, just like Solomon's temple. Participants call upon the four quarters (or spirits) of the North, South, East, and West, which have corresponding elements: earth, air, fire, and water. In some Catholic as well as Enochian angelic traditions, there are four angels that hold specific jobs and represent these directions and elements: Michael, Rafael, Uriel, and Gabriel.

Both Christian and pagan traditions have altars, churches, and fellowship that gives strength. At the end of Wiccan ceremonies, cakes and ale are served. The cakes are made from the grains of the earth to represent the body of the goddess, while the ale acts as the fluid which sustains us—that is, the blood. The ritual counterfeits Holy Communion, which commemorates the body and blood of Christ. The Wiccans' god is seasonally killed and then reborn via the maiden form of the goddess. Jesus was born of the Virgin Mary and then ritually killed before returning from the dead. We enjoy the anointing of the Holy Spirit for certain missions when we invite Him to enter and live within us. Pagans have a ritual called "drawing down the moon" during which they invoke the goddess to enter into them, live within them, and give them power to do missions as they see fit.

In Christianity, we speak in tongues, and there are some who can understand tongues, as mentioned in the Bible (see the list of spiritual gifts in First Corinthians chapter 12). Witchcraft has mediums, who, channel spirits. These spirits speak in tongues that are then interpreted by other mediums or oracles within the group. In Christianity, we practice the laying on of hands to cure physical and spiritual maladies; witches practice energy healing that not only appears the same but is often exactly the same in practice. Christians are instructed to prophecy words from the Father. These words are given for edification, warning, and consolation (see 1 Cor. 14:3). Witches use tools such as runes and Tarot cards to divine the same things from familiar spirits.

We have prayers and psalms with which we call out to our God and ask for His intervention in worldly and personal affairs. Witches bring the same sort of concerns to sabbats, where they offer them up to their god and goddess, ask for intervention, and work spells to actively and personally loose things. They do not wait for answers; they simply do what they can in order to get what they want. Of course, there are strings attached, but there are also other spells to cast in order to offset these side effects.

Again, the only difference—and I can't stress this enough—is who receives your allegiance. In fact, this *should* be the only difference between us and them. They know how to do what we were born to do. We have forgotten that Jesus said, *"Anyone who has faith in Me will do what I have been doing. He will do even greater things than these, because I am going to the Father"* (John 14:12).

Those involved in Wicca need the light, and we must flip on the light switch so that they might be returned to the sheepfold. They would be instantly better-trained than "churched" Christians; yet instead of seeing them as valid, highly-trained special ops soldiers who belong to a different army, most Christians see them as devil worshippers—and tell them so. The problem is that Wiccans don't think of themselves as having anything to do with the devil. So we make fools of ourselves as we stand there and tell them that their swords and shields are fake and their skills are imaginary. In actuality, it is the Christian's stolen sword and shield and the skills that the Lord intended for him that the enemy will kill him with. The pagans have our inheritance. We have given it to them. It's time to take it back. It's time to stop limiting the Holy Spirit regarding what we think He can do for us and what is comfortable for us. No one ever said that doing the right thing is comfortable. It's time to stop insulting the Father by shunning the gifts and skills we have been offered because we don't recognize them as holy. Moreover, there is something even more important that the modern Church doesn't recognize—and that is Jesus.

REDEEMING HIS BRIDE

Here is Rebekah's (Esther's) story, in her own words. Rebekah's (Esther's) story was first told in Darren Wilson's film, *Furious Love*. At the time, Rebekah went by the name "Esther" to protect her identity.

My name is Rebekah (Esther), and I'm 27 years old. I'm going to tell you a little about what I have gone through and what is really going on today. Anton LaVey is not only the writer of *The Satanic Bible* but also the founder of the first satanic church in San Francisco. About 28 years ago, while doing his normal daily activities, he fell into a trance, and during that trance he saw a vision. In the vision, he saw many things that he would need to do and events that were going to happen, one of which involved the fall of one of the five brides of satan. The satanic church has many rules, one of which is that no one is allowed to have sexual intercourse or other sexual contact with a man or woman outside the coven. The repercussions for doing such a thing are very harsh, depending on one's position and level. This particular bride was going to fall, and someone would have to take her place.

Then LaVey saw a child being born in a hospital; he also saw the name of the child and the place where she lived. It was me that he saw. So LaVey immediately sent his workers, including his high priests, to infiltrate the hospital and get the necessary arrangements in motion regarding the upbringing of the child who was about to be born. Because I wasn't "blue blood" or "royal blood" (that is, from a satanic family bloodline), it would be difficult to raise me with my parents around. They would have to infiltrate not only my neighborhood but also my school. Therefore, by the time I was born, some of the doctors and nurses were warlocks and high priestesses so that the proper and necessary incantations and spells could be carried out.

When I was about four years old, a high priest (Keith) and his girlfriend were my in-house nannies, watching my sibling and me. They taught me how to move objects without touching them by using the powers with which I had been born. My element was fire, so I was very drawn to and fond of fire, and I could control it with ease.

One day, I was doing what normal little four-year-old girls do, playing in the basement with my toys. That's when I felt the touch of a hand and heard a voice behind me saying, "Rebekah (Esther), it is time." I turned around and was raped.

I was horrified, but I honestly didn't know that it wasn't normal to be sexually violated. As far as I knew, it was normal. I cried a lot, and when my parents asked me what had gone on and why I was crying, I told them that my "pee-pee" hurt and that Keith had done it. Of course they were horrified, and of course they called the police. The police came over and asked me some questions about what had happened and where Keith had touched me. I told them. I heard later that he was arrested. However, the satanists continued to have access to me through other babysitters and nannies.

From that point on, things progressed very rapidly for me because of the transfer of anointing that had occurred. On a numerical scale, my giftings had increased from a "2" to a "70." I could not only control objects but also could make sure that, if I didn't want someone to touch me, he or she stayed away. By my ninth year, I saw my first "up close and personal" human sacrifice. I saw the locations in some states (some of them in underground caverns) where ceremonies were carried out and where humans were held before being sacrificed. I won't go into detail about the babies because it is much too intense.

The satanic church is much like the Church today, with roundtable discussions about topics such as plans, upcoming events, problems, and problem-causers. There are talks concerning what needs to be infiltrated and what needs to be completely destroyed. I witnessed these discussions. I remember being ten and hearing a certain woman's name mentioned. You see, there was a list of people that was often read; it was a hit list, a list of people to "erase." This name was brought up over and over again. The roundtable members kept asking, "What should we do about this Angela lady?" I finally grew so irritated by this topic that I stood up and said, "I guess you should just kill her. What's the big deal? Run her off the road. She's just a human."

A high priest called General David Weinstin stood up, looked down at me, and said, "Little Rebekah (Esther), you'll soon find out that some people are untouchable. If there's an opening, we have them. But she doesn't have an opening. It's like a law or an incantation—'you can't touch them.'" He sat back down. The authority with which he had spoken impacted me and caused me to shut my mouth immediately.

After Weinstin told me this, I mulled over the phrase—"If there's an opening." Over and over and over, in my mind, I looked for the opening—the soft spot, the weakness. I knew, for example, that if I could find the weakness within a church, we could infiltrate it and take it down. Ninety-nine percent of the time, if a church was successful in the Kingdom of God , a satanist was sent in. Most of the time this person became an elder or even an associate pastor. This is why it is important to pray and fast and to cover and seal the work that the Lord does in a church. You must also stay humble and ensure that Jesus is the only shining star so that you are completely covered.

One Halloween, we were really going through the sacrifices, and the screams of the children were quickly getting to me. So I was given a hard drug. I don't know which one it was, but I remember that all my nerve endings went completely numb, and I couldn't hear the screams of the children anymore. Suddenly, just before the others invited lucifer to come and show himself, I saw entities. I know now that they were angels. I saw them from the shoulders up, and they were surrounding me. I saw these beings all the time, along with auras and demons, but this time they were very close.

Lucifer, who looked like a Spanish prince, appeared. He is not a red creature who carries a pitchfork. He is extremely beautiful, and everything around him is electric and very alluring. But his eyes are pure evil.

The priest gave me communion, which consisted of sperm, blood, and a black widow spider. It wasn't my first communion experience, but it was the third of nine initiations before taking the place of the fifth bride. The priest brought me to the prince, who said, "Soon, Rebekah (Esther), you will take the place of the fifth bride, and then you will belong to me." After that, exhaustion and the drugs took their toll. I passed out, and when I woke, I was in a room and was wearing a new robe. This one had incantations sewn into the sleeves. It was made of black silk and blood-red velvet.

My friend Carolyn (who had been recruited into the group as well) walked into the room. She seemed very excited as she said, "It's tattoo time, Rebekah (Esther)!" It was time for me to take the mark of the bride, and since fire was my element, my mark was a fire tattoo. The objective was that, everywhere I went, people would know in both the natural and the spirit what authority I had and who I was. I got the tattoo, and then I cut my hair, which was down to my waist. It was given to the others and placed in the Ark which is a story for another time.

I was not truly happy. Everything that happened was part of a power trip that was very real and yet also seemed unreal. Everything was bland and cold. Yet it was nice to have so much power. I guess this is why people stay.

Even so, nothing had flavor or taste. It was like taking a drink and not experiencing the feeling of wetness. To make a long story short, I began to skip more and more meetings and masses. *What's the worst they can do?* I thought. *They can't kill me, they can't touch me, and most meetings are boring anyway.*

Soon, the others decided I needed some hands-on experience to get me motivated again, so two of them took me to a Benny Hinn crusade at the stadium in Tacoma, Washington. I was about 16 at the time. I'll never forget it. We were seated on the right-hand side of the stadium in the nosebleed section, in the middle of the row. The place was packed and noisy. I was instructed to curse Mr. Hinn. There was pure white light around him like a ball. It was amazing. I thought, *Is this a joke?* You simply don't curse people who are surrounded by pure white light in either the satanic or the new age culture. White represents power, so I assumed Mr. Hinn was like a wizard. *You don't mess with wizards or you get killed*, I thought. To top it off, those "angel creatures" were all over the platform.

Nevertheless, I did what I'd been told to do. Suddenly, Benny Hinn stopped what he was doing and pointed to where we were sitting. He said, "You three devil worshippers, stop cursing me and this meeting."

See, we're in trouble, I thought. He continued to point at us as he said, "You in the middle—you're going to be getting saved soon… And you other two—turn to Jesus or your souls will be going to hell."

Then he addressed the crowd: "Let the people of God pray right now for their salvation." Everyone began stretching their hands toward our section. I suddenly felt like I was being electrocuted. I began to scream, and then I blacked out.

After this experience, I started to contemplate why we were involved in this power trip, trying to control everything around us. A few weeks passed by, and I still couldn't get the evening at the stadium out of my head.

One day, while I was deep in thought, Carolyn (who was 18 or 19 at the time) called me out of the blue. She was sobbing. "I want out, Rebekah (Esther)." I didn't fully understand what she meant by "wanting out." I tried to tell her everything would be OK.

"Just calm down. If you want out, it'll be OK. I'll make sure nothing happens. It's not like you know anything special or you're too high up." (Carolyn wasn't as experienced as I was, nor was she at the same level.)

"I guess you're right," she said. "But you've told me things."

"It's OK. It's not like I've told you locations and times." Carolyn started to cry again. "Where are you?" I asked.

"I'll SMS it to you," she answered. About 45 minutes later, she sent me an address. I found the place and knocked on the door. An older man answered and said, "You must be Carolyn's friend. She's locked the door and isn't letting any of us in. Funny thing is, I didn't know that door had a lock." I ignored the man and others who were in the house and proceeded to Carolyn's room. The door to the room that was supposedly locked opened without my touching it and then closed again.

"Who are these people?" I asked Carolyn, who was crying so hard that she could barely speak. I slapped her in her face and shook her. "Stop it, Carolyn!" I cried. "It'll be OK.... I won't let them touch you. It'll be OK, really."

A car pulled up at the curb at the front of the house, but no one got out. I looked out the window and felt a chill run down my spine. "I'll deal with this," I said. "Let me talk to them."

As I headed toward the door, Carolyn flew backward and hit the wall. The occupants of the car had astro-projected themselves into the room and now proceeded to beat Carolyn right in front of me. I tried to protect her, but I couldn't move at all. I was infuriated, and I was powerless. I was forced to watch as my friend was being beaten up. After battering Carolyn continually for a full ten minutes, they left.

Carolyn's face was unrecognizable. The man who had answered the door had heard the noise and had been trying to get through the door the whole time. His face turned white when he saw the mess in the room. "Young lady, what's happened here?" he demanded. "What did you do?"

I was in a dream state. "I have to go," I said. "I'm sorry.... Call an ambulance."

"You're not going anywhere," he said.

"I didn't do anything," I protested. "I have to go. You'd never understand." I ran out of the house.

Carolyn was in a coma. A few days later, she died, and something inside me snapped. I thought, *Who cares about all your meetings and power trips?! Who cares if you're in the government, society, politics, and schools? You killed my friend—for what?*

That week, *The Blair Witch Project* was released in theaters, and I thought it looked interesting. I went to the theater to see it. In reality, it's a pathetic film, and everyone dies in the end. And yet, as I sat in the movie theater watching the end of the film, I felt a thick, heavy veil being taken off my head. For the first time ever and for just a split second, I could think for myself—without the influence of the demons that were around me and inside me. It felt like a split-second breath of fresh air after being under a pile of heavy blankets for hours.

This isn't good, I thought. *I have to get out. This movie isn't real, but I'm going to wind up like those kids—dead. Eventually, I'm to screw something up in the coven, and I'll be sacrificed on a slab of stone. I've got to get out. I've got to get out—move away, and get the hell out.*

I knew that now that I had entertained the idea, the others would know because of the deep soul ties we had. I knew this as soon as I made the conscious decision to leave. They'd find out, and they would try to kill me. I was terrified. But then I saw a lady's face in my mind's eye. *Who's that?* I wondered.

Then I remembered. Her name was Pamela. My mother had suffered a nervous breakdown and had tried to kill herself. She went away for five months and lived in a trailer behind this woman's house. I thought, *If she survived, then so can I.* What I didn't know is that Jesus had impressed Pamela's face upon me, knowing it would lead to my deliverance and to the reason I'm alive today.

I went home, packed everything I could carry in a duffle bag, and dialed Pamela's number. She picked up the phone.

"Hey, I know you, but you don't know me really well," I started. "But I've had a situation come up, and I need to move out of my house right now. Would it be OK to come to your house till I can figure something out?"

Pamela responded, "Sure, it'll be OK. I was just praying for you and your family." I didn't catch the word "praying." All I was thinking about was that I had to get out and get away before they came to get me. I went to the train station in Vancouver, Washington and got off the train a few hours later at the Tacoma station.

I was so frightened. I remember doing "invisible incantations" so they couldn't see where I was going— even though I knew it would be useless since I was praying all by myself. I didn't have any reinforcements—no friends or family who would even begin to understand what was happening.

When I saw Pamela, all I could do was cry like a baby. She gathered my things and put me in the car. I explained a little of the situation as she drove. When we got to her house and drove onto her property, I stepped out of the car and started to draw a bloodline by saying a sort of protection incantation. I cut the palm of my hand diagonally and, as the blood dripped down, I walked the border of her property. Then I looked behind me, and she was doing the same thing—but in the way that Christians do, with salt and olive oil. She, too, was chanting a weird spell. I later realized she had been speaking in tongues.

I didn't sleep at all for many weeks. I was tormented. Every time I ventured out, off the property, I was constantly looking behind my back. I was always extremely paranoid. It was horrible. I saw them everywhere. It was terribly frightening. Every so often, they left a sign at the edge of the property, like a calling card: "We know you're here." This went on for two months. My presence began to take a heavy toll on the family. One of them would walk into a room, and it would instantly become ice cold. Things flew across rooms. And then there were the sleepless nights.

Finally, Pamela called her friend Joanna and explained the situation. Joanna mentioned a woman named Angela, who did deliverances. So Joanna called Angela and explained my situation to her. I would realize later that Angela was the lady who had been mentioned so frequently at the roundtables. It's amazing how God connects everything.

"I know about Rebekah (Esther)," Angela said. "I've seen her, and I know what she's into and what she's been through. I'll do the deliverance, but this is a major deliverance. I want you to fast and pray for a week—'cause this isn't a light thing at all."

After a week, I was completely exhausted. On the day that I was to receive prayer (at Joanna's house), I did a protective spell with a circle of stones and took one last dose of heroine. I didn't really look to see how much heroin I was taking.

Joanna and I got in the car to go to what I like to call my "final destination." For the first time ever, I saw more than just the shoulders up of one of the figures I'd seen so many times before. This time, I saw a full-blown angel. He was massive.

I've overdosed, I thought. *But if I'm going to die, it'll be OK because at least I'll die in peace.* I saw not only the massive angel but a whole host of them riding with us and actually driving us to my final destination. It was very frightening and nice at the same time. I tried to jump out of the car, but the massive angel kept me inside.

We drove for about 20 minutes, which seemed like forever to me. As we drove onto the property, I saw only white—and then a prism of lights joining the angels, who looked as though they were waiting for a war to begin. They looked so serious. Without touching it, I opened the door and exited the car. I walked into the house, and the door flew open without my touching it. Angela caught the door as she said, "I don't think so,

Babe." And she added, "Oh, don't worry about that guy [referring to the massive angel]; he's my angel."

I was immensely relieved and shocked at the same time. I hadn't met many seers before, so this was really nice. As I walked in, I saw that Joanna had prepared her house for a massive invasion of demonic forces. She had taped the cupboards shut and put sheets all over the couches and chairs. *What is going on here?* I thought.

The first thing we did was sit down, and as we did so, everyone was quietly chanting in that weird language that Pamela had used. I felt like my nerves were on top of my skin, and I had a difficult time sitting still. I was very angry for no reason at all.

I had all my garb on—all my rings and necklaces and everything else that would protect me or have an effect on my atmosphere. Angela was asking Pamela about me. I was in what felt like a drunken stupor. I couldn't respond to a lot of things. I just stared at this Angela lady as I figured out that she was the very one we had been trying to destroy. I was confused and full of rage. She was so loving, and yet she had authority like no one I had ever met. She talked to me in my mind even as she spoke verbally with Pamela and Joanna. I was trembling inside, trying to prevent the demons from taking over and killing the women.

Angela told me dates and locations and names that no one ever should have known—no one except a satanist, that is. And then she looked down at her watch and said, "Look, Babe, I've got a plane to catch. You have two choices: you can allow Jesus to come in and save you, or you can allow lucifer—satan—to take your soul and drag it to hell. Which will it be?"

I was shocked. No one had ever talked to me in that tone of voice. And no one had ever given me an ultimatum before. I couldn't hold the demons back; they were taking over. But with everything inside me, I screamed, "Please, help me!"

Angela put oil on my forehead in the shape of a cross and said, "In the name of the Father, the Son, and the Holy Spirit." I blacked out. All I remember is waking up and feeling like 90 percent of my body was missing. I was so empty. Everything was gone. But then I prayed with Angela, asking the Holy Spirit to come inside me.

I got utterly drunk in the Spirit for the first time. It was better than any drug I had ever taken before. And for the first time ever, I heard birds singing. I was in shock; I had read about this. *This is amazing!* I thought. I was like a new person looking through different eyes. I also received a miracle regarding my heroin addiction. After that day, I never had another withdrawal symptom, which is hell in itself. I was completely free. It was the best day of my life. I was finally free, like the butterfly I had always envied. Now I could become a new creation, just like Second Corinthians 5:17 says. I was free! Friday the 13th of August 1999 was the day of my new birth. I was redeemed. There would be a few tough years ahead…but that's another story.

I was free. Free at last, free at last—thank God, I'm free at last.

Rebekah and Angela have made a DVD of Rebekah's story. *Redeeming His Bride* may be purchased at www.angelagreenig.com.

Let's Fight for Freedom!

Notice that the ending of Rebekah's (Esther's) testimony is taken from a quote by Dr. Martin Luther King, Jr., who had a dream as he fought against the tyranny of injustice. He prayed, and God gave him an army of every race, creed, and color to fight against racism and to bring equality. As believers, we must fight to bring justice for all for the glory of God's Kingdom. Throughout history, many lives have been lost—but even after death they have left behind a blueprint for you and me to follow. We *can* give hope to those lost and bound in endless darkness. We *are* the crusaders.

If you don't understand the world of the enemy, however, it will be difficult to do battle and to win. Remember: *"Our struggle is not against flesh and blood, but against the rulers, against the authorities, against the powers of this dark world and against the spiritual forces of evil in the heavenly realms"* (Eph. 6:12).

No general has ever gone into battle and won without knowing his enemy. We are in a war for our families, for our children, and for our very existence as Christians. In the United States we are fighting for the Ten Commandments, freedom of speech, and the privilege to pray and share Jesus. Our rights are being violated! Why? We have allowed the enemy to creep in. Now, due to our complacency and fear, darkness is eating at the very fabric of society—yet I believe that this will be our finest hour. When the going gets tough, the tough get going!

Let us learn to discern the times we are in...let us take up our cross. Let's heed the call to rescue as many as possible out of darkness and bring them into the glorious light— let's get ready!

EPILOGUE

This book may have been a true eye-opener for some of you. My desire is that God's glory would pierce through the darkness and open your spiritual eyes to see the truth. I'm sure this book, along with my other books, *Armed & Dangerous: Basic Training* and *Demons & Angels: And the Origins Thereof*, will be great weapons to use in defeating the enemy.

It is only through the written Word of our King and His precious blood that we have access to the throne room of the true and living God. We all have dominion and authority, as given to us by Jesus, to subdue and destroy the works of darkness, as well as loose the chains that have kept many imprisoned.

This is the time for the spoken word of the Lord to be declared and released. FREEDOM!

My prayer is that a holy Army will arise from their tombs, take off their grave clothes of sorrow and separation, be ignited by a holy, blazing fire, and be like the voice of John the Baptist crying out in the wilderness, "Prepare ye the way of the Lord!"

Hold on…God's coming!

Till the End,
Angela

ENDNOTES

1. Metaphysics 101, "The Dead Sea Scrolls," http://www.paganspath.com/meta/deadsea.htm

2. http://www.jta.org/news/article/2010/01/25/1010299/report-anti-semtism-up-dramatically-in-2009

3. http://idfspokesperson.com/facts-figures/rocket-attacks-toward-israel

4. http://wordinfo.info/unit/629/page:2

5. http://www.tititudorancea.org/z/secret_society.htm

6. http://www.eurekaencyclopedia.com/index.php/Category:Worship_Of_Demons

7. Webster's Revised Unabridged Dictionary (1913).

8. Vexen Crabtree, "The Aspect of Lucifer," <http://www.dpjs.co.uk/lucifer.html>

9. The Gospel of Thomas. Translations by Thomas O. Lambin, B.P. Grenfell & A.S. Hunt, and Bentley Layton. Commentary by Craig Schenk. http://www.sacred-texts.com/chr/thomas.htm

10. Anton Szandor LaVey, *The Satanic Bible* (New York: HarperCollins, 1976), 9.

11. Lawrence Sutin, *Do What Thou Wilt* (New York: St. Martin's Press, 2000), 38.

12. http://www.thelema101.com/intro

13. http://heru-ra-ha.tripod.com/topics/goetia.html

14. Stephen Skinner & David Rankine, *The Goetia of Dr. Rudd* (Singapore: Golden Hoard Press, 2007) 47-50.

15. http://theisticsatanism.com/geifodd/mysticism.html

16. Summers, Montague. *The History of Witchcraft* (New York: First Carol Publishing, 1993), 118-133.

17. *La Sorcière: The Witch of the Middle Ages*, translated by L. J. Teotter, "The only Authorized English Translation" (London, 1863).

18. Religious Doctrine Dictionary, http://www.wearethevine.com/religions/index.htm

19. Manly P. Hall, *The Secret Teachings of All Ages* (Radford, VA: Wilder Publications, 2009), 20.

20. http://www.fbi.gov/about-us/cjis/ncic/ncic-missing-person-and-unidentified-person-statistics-for-2010

21. Leonard R.N. Ashley, *The Complete Book of Devils and Demons* (New York: Skyhorse Publishing, 2006) ch. 3.

22. http://www.witchcraftandwitches.com/related_satanism.html

23. http://en.wikipedia.org/wiki/Friday_the_13th

24. http://unofficialnetworks.com/2012/01/13/friday-13ththe-knights-templar-goddess-frigga/
25. http://www.optionmonster.com/drj_blog/article.php?page=drj_blog/how_davinci_code_national_treasure_play_into_friday_the_13th_48050.html

26. Gilmore/Satanism: Peter H. Gilmore, "Satanism: The Feared Religion," http://www.churchofsatan.com/Pages/Feared.html

27. Gilmore Interview: Wikinews, "Satanism: An Interview with Church of Satan High Priest Peter Gilmore," http://en.wikinews.org/wiki/Satanism:_An_interview_with_Church_of_Satan_High_Priest_Peter_Gilmore

28. Point of Inquiry: Point of Inquiry with D. J. Grothe, "Peter H. Gilmore—Science and Satanism," http://www.pointofinquiry.org/peter_h_gilmore_science_and_satanism/

29. http://people.usd.edu/~clehmann/pir/asiamysi.htm

30. Webster's Online Dictionary, "Tetramorph," <//www.websters-online-dictionary.org/Te/Tetramorph.html>

31. www.moonchild.ch/Puzzle/4creaures.html

32. www.archangels-and-angels.com/misc/angelic hierarchy.html

33. Anton Szandor LaVey, *The Satanic Bible* (New York: HarperCollins, 1976).

34. Sins: "The Nine Satanic Sins," <//www.churchofsatan.com/Pages/Sins.html>

35. http://www.angelfire.com/realm/shades/magic/demon.htm

36. Ibid.

37. Ibid.

38. Ibid.

39. Ibid.

40. "Demon," Microsoft® Encarta® Online Encyclopedia 2000. http://encarta.msn.com © 1997-2000 Microsoft Corporation. All rights reserved.

41. http://www.teenwitch.com/magick/castingcircle.html

42. Ibid.

43. http://www.websters-online-dictionary.org/definitions/necromancy

44. http://www.profilingtheunexplained.com/forums/index.php?showtopic=4102

45. http://en.wikipedia.org/wiki/Magician_(paranormal)

46. http://ecumenicalbuddhism.blogspot.com/2008/02/what-hell.html

47. Ibid.

48. http://www.witchcraftandwitches.com/contempo-
rary_wicca.html

ADDITIONAL SOURCES:

The Book of Thoth: A Short Essay on the Tarot of the Egyptians, Being the Equinox Volume III No. V, Aleister Crowley

Do What Thou Wilt: A Life of Aleister Crowley, Lawrence Sutin, Pub.: Macmillan, 2000

The Confessions of Aleister Crowley: An Autohagiography, Aleister Crowley, eds. John Symonds & Kenneth Grant, Pub.: Routledge & Kegan Paul

ANGELA GREENIG MINISTRIES

Angela Greenig is a seasoned seer/warrior for Jesus Christ and a leading force in deliverance ministry. Since July 1983 she has been a Defender of the Faith and a Voice for those who have no voice, traveling the world, preaching and training up the Body of Christ. As Founder of Angela Greenig Ministries, and Kingdom Invasion Media, she has assisted others in their physical and spiritual needs.

Through her travels, Angela has built and contributed to ministries in many cities throughout America and in various nations of the world. She has written and released several books and DVDs to guide and instruct God's people to become armed and dangerous to the enemy. Her videos can be viewed on her "Justice for All" channel at XPmedia.com; and radio broadcasts can be heard on the "Justice Movement" sessions of Seattle's Freedom Radio 1590 AM every Sunday morning.

Her teaching and insight come from years on the front lines of spiritual warfare, with a heart of welfare for the salvation and deliverance of people. Washington State is home for Angela and her husband, Larry; and their ministry is based at the "Eagles Landing" location in Sumner.

www.AngelaGreenig.com
Angela@AngelaGreenig.com
20825 Hwy # 410 E
PMB # 218
Bonney Lake, WA 98391

OTHER RESOURCES
BY ANGELA GREENIG

<u>Books</u>
Armed & Dangerous: Basic Training
Demons & Angels: And the Origins Thereof
Colors & Numbers
The Seer/Prophet/Knower of Our Times

<u>DVDs</u>
Armed & Dangerous
Demons & Angels
Redeeming His Bride
How to Do an Effective Deliverance

<u>Training Set</u>
School of the Gladiator

The above resources can be purchased from www.AngelaGreenig.com

eGenCo

Generation Culture Transformation
Specializing in publishing for generation culture change

Visit us Online at:
www.egen.co
www.goingebook.com

Write to: eGen Co. LLC
824 Tallow Hill Road
Chambersburg, PA 17202 USA
Phone: 717-461-3436
Email: info@egen.co

 facebook.com/egenbooks

youtube.com/egenpub

 egen.co/blog

Printed in Great Britain
by Amazon.co.uk, Ltd.,
Marston Gate.